ACTIONS, STYLES and SYMBOLS in KINETIC FAMILY DRAWINGS (K-F-D)

ACTIONS, STYLES and SYMBOLS in KINETIC FAMILY DRAWINGS (K-F-D)

An Interpretative Manual

By Robert C. Burns
Director, Seattle Institute of Human Development

and S. Harvard Kaufman, M.D.
Clinical Professor of Psychiatry, Department of Psychiatry, University of Washington School of Medicine (Seattle)

BRUNNER/MAZEL • New York

To POLLY
AND
CINDY, HEATHER AND CARTER

Copyright © 1972 by Robert C. Burns and S. Harvard Kaufman

Published by
BRUNNER/MAZEL, INC.
19 Union Square West
New York, N.Y. 10003

Library of Congress Catalog Card No. 70-186854
ISBN 0-87630-228-2

MANUFACTURED IN THE UNITED STATES OF AMERICA

15   14   13   12   11   10

INTRODUCTION

At all too rare an interval a very bright star appears in the projective technique sky. One such was Hermann Rorschach's Ink Blot Test. Burns and Kaufman's Kinetic Family Drawing Test appears to be another. The Rorschach tells us how the individual experiences; the K-F-D how he perceives himself in his family setting. Seldom has a test shown itself to be able to tell us so much about a subject so quickly and so surely.

The Kinetic Family Drawing Test gives me the same feeling as did the Rorschach when it came to this country so many years ago—that it is a tool which is going to be phenomenally useful to us in years to come. I was also much struck by Lowenfeld's Mosaic Test when it was first introduced. The K-F-D is a worthy third in this outstanding company. In using this test, one has the impression of being in near the beginning of what will undoubtedly turn out to be a major projective technique.

This present volume, *Actions, Styles and Symbols in Kinetic Family Drawings: An Interpretative Manual*, is a truly wanted book. It will find a ready, in fact an eager, audience since it provides just that kind of help and information which many readers of the authors' introductory book, *Kinetic Family Drawings (K-F-D)*, have wished for. It fills a real need. A good many clinicians, since the publication of this earlier book, have begun their own collections of family drawings. The wealth of drawings and of interpretations in this present volume will permit these individual collections of drawings to come to life.

Beginning users of the K-F-D inevitably ask themselves, of each drawing they are presented with: *What does it mean? What does it tell us? What is the subject saying about himself and his family?* This book gives many answers. In the richness of its interpretations it provides an intellectual delight. I should warn, "Read this book at your own risk," because once you are really hooked on this test it is hard to get away."

It is generally agreed that the unconscious speaks through symbols. Any adequate interpretation of K-F-D responses, in addition to the surface interpretation which any clinician, however sophisticated, will give to the drawings produced, requires interpretation at the symbolic level. Beds, bicycles, brooms; cats, clowns, cribs; lamps, lawnmowers, leaves; snakes, stars, stop signs, and so on through the alphabet—the authors give their own interesting interpretations of the outstanding symbols commonly used. To mention only one, the elucidation of the "garbage" theme, especially as it relates to the new baby in the family, is of special interest to any professionals, or laymen, concerned with the impact of the new member of the family on that older sibling who is being displaced.

But that these are no dream book interpretations is suggested by the warning that the meaning of symbols can be overinterpreted. The authors warn, correctly, that in any attempt at hypothesizing the unconscious expression of any single symbol one must weigh the alternate and sometimes seemingly incompatible interpretation.

Even more interesting than the authors' interpretation of specific symbols is their elucidation of *styles* of drawing. For instance, the notion of compartmentalization in which the child isolates individual members of the family by putting them in boxlike rectangles, or by encapsulating them, or even by putting some on the back of the page, is especially helpful. (While reading this manuscript, I examined a little girl who not only drew her father on the back of the page, but pictured him as sitting back to at his desk in a high-backed chair, so that only his arm showed.) The authors also give us good, clear interpretations not only of *symbols* and *styles* but also of *themes*. Symbols, styles and themes —all tell their own stories.

The customary actions of father and mother, as seen by subjects, are especially noteworthy. Children see mothers as cooking, washing dishes, making beds; see fathers as working, mowing lawn, playing ball. Young children seem to take these differences in sex role quite for granted, though, in contrast, boys and girls do not seem to see themselves as behaving in substantially different ways. In this connection it is interesting to note the ratio of boys and girls—many more boys than girls—which the authors find in a clinic population. Why is it, we wonder, that boys have so very much harder a time than girls in a society such as our own?

The very generous inclusion of all drawings discussed is extremely useful. Seldom have basic data been provided more generously by a publisher. Every reader is here permitted to draw his own conclusions, make his own interpretations, arrive at his own insights.

This is by no means a book for superficial reading. My own reaction is that I wish to study seriously each drawing and the authors' interpretation of that drawing. I believe that most readers who are really interested in K-F-D will feel the same way. Though on the surface this test might seem to offer a situation in which interpretation might be made fairly easily even by the layman, the present manual, clear as it is, makes one appreciate that the interpretation of human drives and motivation is by no means simple. The K-F-D analysis sheet offers a useful beginning objective measure of this highly subjective and individualized test response.

Anyone using the K-F-D test can enjoy the excitement of being in at the beginning of a marvellously effective new way of measuring human behavior. The years ahead offer much promise for this new technique. The Kinetic Family Drawing Test can make a real contribution to any clinician's battery of projective techniques. I predict that this test will have a great future among those professionals whose work focuses on an understanding, and interpretation, of drawings of children—those drawings which can and do tell us so very much about what children are like, what their problems are, what life looks like to them. This new book by Burns and Kaufman is one of the most important and potentially useful which I have ever read. I recommend it very highly.

LOUISE BATES AMES, PH.D., *Chief Psychologist*
Gesell Institute of Child Development
Formerly, President of the Society
for Projective Techniques

CONTENTS

x

xiii

PREFACE

This book is about the actions, styles and symbols appearing in children's kinetic (action) drawings of their families. The technique of obtaining children's drawings by asking them to "draw everyone in the family doing something" has been discussed in *Kinetic Family Drawings (K-F-D)* by Burns and Kaufman (5).

Kinetic Family Drawings (K-F-D) was meant to be a general introduction to a new tool for understanding children, particularly troubled children. Our aim in the introductory book was to communicate the excitement of working with a new clinical tool. While the book was structured in a developmental and partially Freudian framework, it was hoped the children's K-F-D's would "speak for themselves" with a freshness and a minimum of interference from the greybeard authors.

The aim of this book is to point out the K-F-D actions, styles and symbols which slowly came into focus during a dozen years of scrutiny by the authors as they gradually accumulated some 10,000 K-F-D's from individual patients. Descriptive notes on the drawings were written by the examiner as directed by the patient.

While it is hoped the K-F-D's will continue to "speak for themselves," the authors will try to communicate some of the characteristics of the K-F-D which slowly emerged for them.

Grateful thanks is expressed to Anaxagoras of Clazomenae (500-428 B.C.) whose definition of Understanding (NOUS) — *"giving movement, unity and system to what had previously been a jumble of inert elements"*—provided the intellectual spark touching off our K-F-D investigations.

Thanks, also, to Dolores Goodell McCarthy for her skillful efforts in preparing the manuscript and for her joyous enthusiasm.

Our thanks, above all, to the troubled children who did the K-F-D's. May their pictured pleas for understanding and love, often so simply and trustingly portrayed, be better understood and answered by all of us.

ROBERT C. BURNS
S. HARVARD KAUFMAN

CHAPTER 1

CHILDREN'S DRAWINGS

I. INTRODUCTION

Children's drawings have a freshness and naivete which is too quickly lost as conformity, defensiveness, and sophistication take over. It is during this period of openness and freshness that children tell us much about themselves and the human condition.

Bender (3) and Despert (8) have pioneered in the psychological interpretation of the art of disturbed children. Anastasi and Foley (2) made an early exhaustive survey of the literature concerning artistic behavior in the abnormal. Alschuler and Hattwick (1) contributed to the appreciation of children's painting. Raven (21) described an imaginative technique in which the child was asked to draw and, while drawing, to imagine and describe a series of events.

More recently, Di Leo (9) has discussed children's art with emphasis on developmental and deviant characteristics. The comprehensive work of Koppitz (17) has focused on a systematic evaluation of multiple aspects of human figure drawings of children age five to twelve. Dennis (7) has studied group values through children's drawings.

II. ANALYSIS OF HUMAN FIGURE DRAWINGS AS PSYCHOLOGICAL TESTS

A. *Draw-a-Person Test (D-A-P)*

In 1926, Florence Goodenough published *"Measurement of Intelligence by Drawings"* (12). A child was told to "Draw a Person," and the drawings were scored for mental age by a quantitative method. The Goodenough D-A-P test soon became an accepted and widely used psychological test of intelligence.

B. *House-Tree-Person Test (H-T-P)*

Buck (4) introduced the House-Tree-Person (H-T-P) test in 1948. A child was asked to draw a house, a tree and a person. Clinical interpretations of the drawings were made. The H-T-P was one of the first uses of human figure drawings as a psychological projective test. Catalogs such as that of Jolles' (16) describe in great detail the symbolic interpretations of the house, the tree and the person.

C. *Draw-a-Family Test (D-A-F)*

The earliest report found in the literature on family drawings (D-A-F) are those by Hulse (14) (15). Aside from studies by Reznikoff and Reznikoff (22) and Shearn and Russell (23), no other reports of the D-A-F could be found in the journal literature. Hammer (13), Koppitz (17), and Di Leo (9) discuss the use of D-A-F in their comprehensive books.

D. *Kinetic-Family-Drawings (K-F-D)*

In 1970 Burns and Kaufman described a method of simply asking children to draw the members of their families *doing* things. It was hoped that the addition of movement to the akinetic drawings would help mobilize a child's feelings not only as related to Self concept but also in the area of interpersonal relations.

The K-F-D often reflects primary disturbances much more quickly and adequately than interviews or other probing techniques. For example, 6-year-old Doug was causing a great disturbance at school and at home. Doug produced K-F-D 1.

Note the three hearts adjacent to the supine "Dad" and the proximity of Doug to him. The father had a history of three seri-

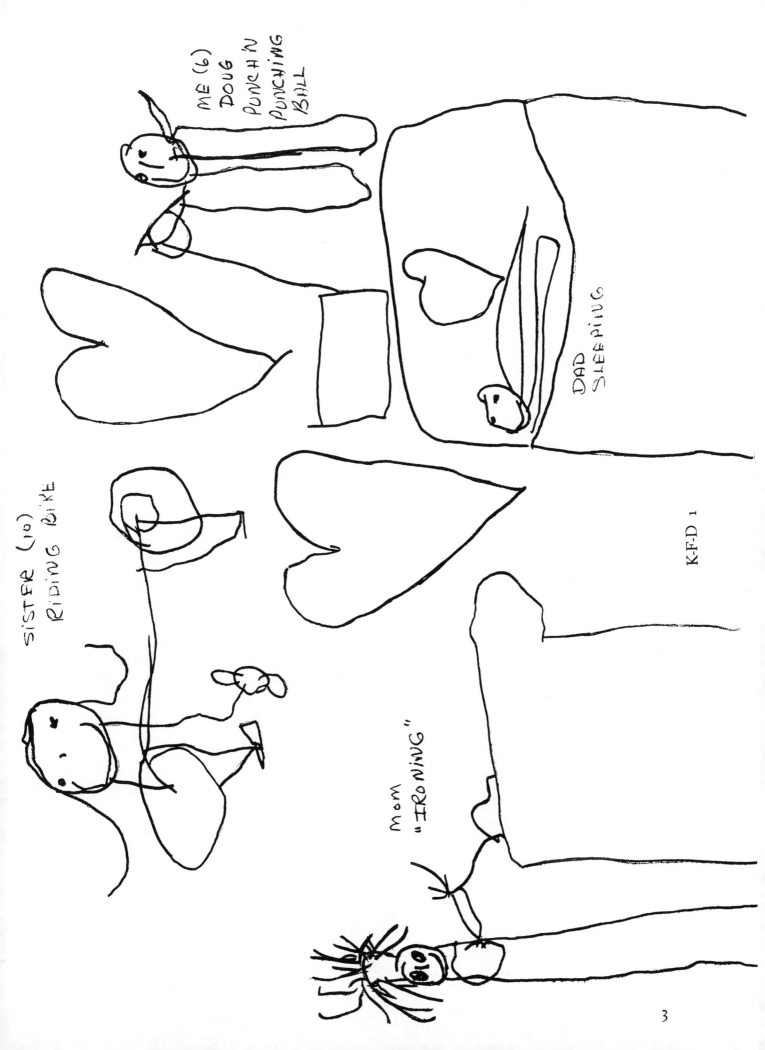

ME (6)
DOUG
PUNCH'N
PUNCHING
BALL

DAD
SLEEPING

SISTER (10)
RIDING BIKE

MOM
"IRONING"

K-F-D 1

3

ous heart attacks in the past nine months. The "*symbols*" of the hearts have obvious validity. The "*style*" of encapsulating and underlining the father reflects Doug's concern and focus of attention on Dad. The·"*actions*" are related to Doug's feelings. His own *action*, "punching," reflects his rage against the forces which have struck down his Dad. The *action* of the mother, "ironing," reflects Doug's need for warmth from her—intensified by Dad's inability to give warmth. Dad's *action* is "sleeping"—reflecting his illness and impotency. The sister's *action* is "riding a bike"—a normal activity suggesting Doug's "normal" feelings toward her.

Through Doug's portrayal and through our analysis of his K-F-D actions, styles and symbols, we improve our understanding of Doug and his behavior.

Before embarking on our exploration of the K-F-D's produced by troubled children, let us consider a few produced by "normal" children.

4

CHAPTER 2

NORMAL KINETIC FAMILY DRAWINGS

I. PROCEDURE FOR OBTAINING K-F-D's

The drawings are obtained from children individually. The child is asked to seat himself on a small chair at a table of appropriate height. A sheet of plain white, 8½ x 11 inch paper is placed on the table directly in front of him. A No. 2 pencil is placed in the center of the paper and he is asked to *"Draw a picture of everyone in your family, including you, DOING something. Try to draw whole people, not cartoons or stick people. Remember, make everyone DOING something—some kind of action."*

The examiner then leaves the room and checks back periodically. The situation is terminated when the child indicates verbally or by gesture that he is finished. No time limit is given. Non-compliance is extremely rare. If the child says, *"I can't,"* he is encouraged periodically and left in the room until he completes the K-F-D.

II. K-F-D's PRODUCED BY "WELL ADJUSTED" OR "NORMAL" CHILDREN

K-F-D 2, made by 8½-year-old Liz, shows a family with no barriers between the members and a physical closeness. There is a light shining above, which often in our drawings depicts a general warmth. One has the feeling in looking at this drawing of a close relationship between the parents and between the parents and the children.

BROTHER

DAD

K-F-D 2

Mon)

SELF (8)

7

K-F-D 3, by 9-year-old Jim, again reflects closeness in the family. This time, the activities of the parents are included in the total feeling. The mother is nurturing the family through her cooking activities; the father is close to Jim and is turning on the light. One has the feeling of happiness and closeness between members of the family in the total family atmosphere and activity.

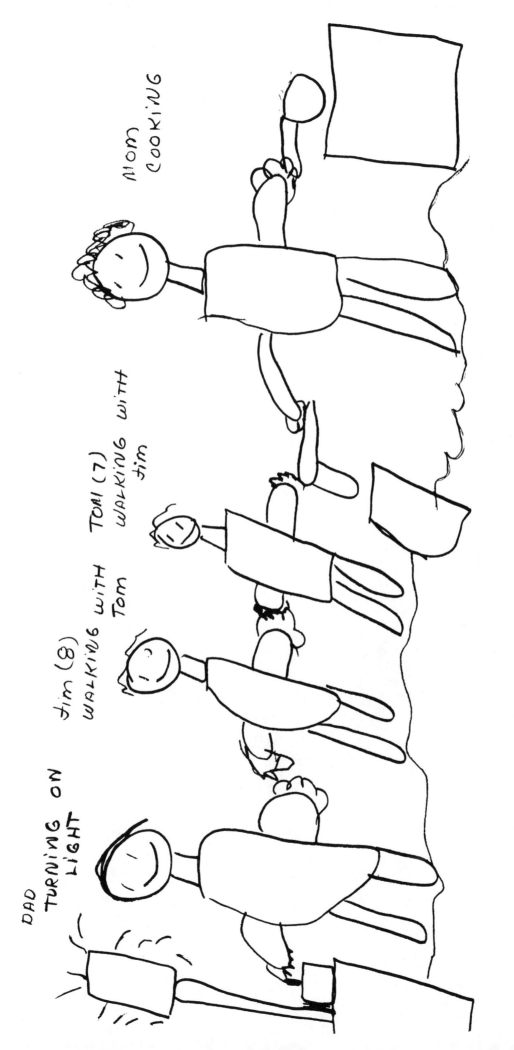

MOM
COOKING

TOM (7)
WALKING WITH
JIM

JIM (8)
WALKING WITH
TOM

DAD
TURNING ON
LIGHT

K-F-D 3

9

K-F-D 4, by 11-year-old Peter, reflects a closeness in the family. They are all being photographed; the beam of the light is on them. There are no barriers between members of the family.

K-F-D 4

11

In K-F-D 5, we see a typical adolescent drawing by 13½-year-old Joe, who is beginning to assert his independence, which, of course, is quite natural at this age.

We see the "handy" mother cooking for the family, albeit she looks somewhat stern—many parents seem stern to teenagers.

The 11-year-old sister is busy talking to her friend on the telephone. The hardworking father is asleep. The television is the center of the family with the rather disgruntled Joe looking at it, but one gets the feeling that he would rather be "doing his own thing." Grandpa is in the corner playing cards and is somewhat isolated by distance and the table from the others in the family.

If we look at the drawing more carefully, perhaps we can "see" more. If, for example, we look at the relative heights of the family members, we see that the father is the ascendant person. We are reminded of the ancient dictum that one's head must not appear above that of the King. While the father is asleep, he seems to be the dominant person in the "pecking order"—his head is next to the lamp with the light theme so frequent in our drawings. On the other hand, the bottom person in the pecking order is Grandpa, who is obviously not dominant in the family. Joe places himself close to but below the father and seems to be impatiently awaiting his own "rise." The mother is close to but "over" the daughter, who seems preoccupied with her own peer group connections outside the home. The symbolism of the bed as related to the sister and the controls suggested by the hypervigilant mother are part of Joe's pubertal world.

This drawing, then, depicts "normal" adolescent strivings in an assertive but well-controlled young male who has identified with and grudgingly accepted the "temporary" authority of the parents.

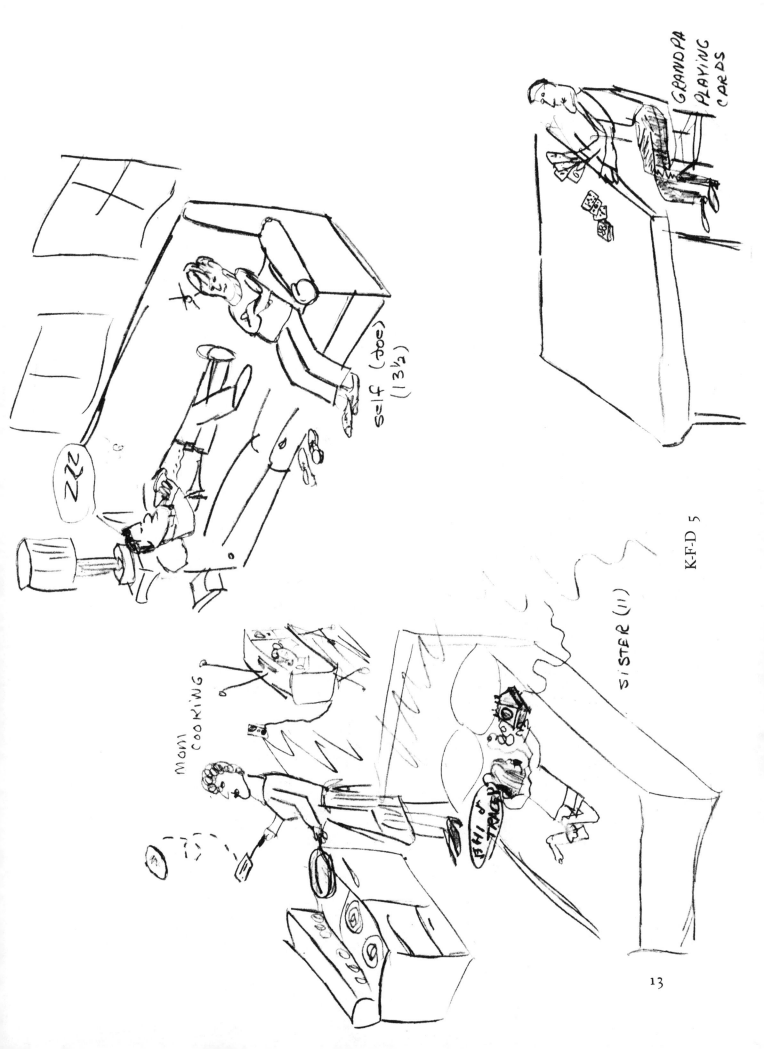

self (Joe)
(13½)

zzz

GRANDPA
PLAYING
CARDS

MOM
COOKING

SISTER (11)

K-F-D 6, by 12½-year-old Anne, reflects the blooming independence of adolescence. However, the conflicts depicted begin to deviate from normalcy. One notes the peaceful central figure of the father, who is dominant although apparently overworked. The mother is busy in the kitchen, but she is "faceless." Anne is busy reading, with her head turned away from the family, and she is absorbed in her own world.

One wonders about the distorted, open-mouthed 14-year-old brother, who is "above" Anne. The brother's figure was larger but was erased. The felt rejection of the mother and conflict with the brother are significant problem areas for Anne.

As we view Anne's K-F-D, we "see" much more if we are familiar with the "meaningful" aspects of individual human figure drawings (H-F-D's). Machover (19) (20), described some of the qualitative features in H-F-D's. For those not familiar with works such as Machover's, a brief summary of H-F-D characteristics and their common clinical interpretation is given in the Appendix.

Analysis of individual H-F-D's may be done "in vacuo." However, analysis of individual K-F-D figures calls for an interpretation within the matrix of the total drawing. Some recurrent characteristics of individual K-F-D figures are worth considering before focusing on actions, styles and symbols.

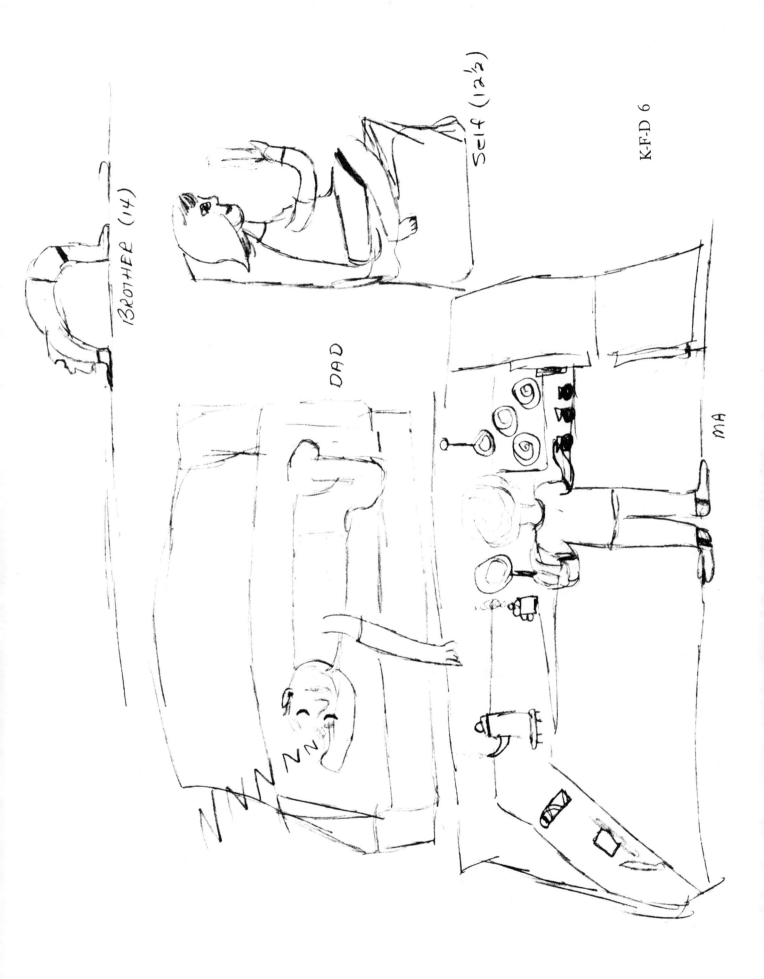

BROTHER (14)

DAD

Self (12½)

MA

K-F-D 6

15

CHAPTER 3

CHARACTERISTICS OF INDIVIDUAL K-F-D FIGURES

A. *Arm Extensions*

Arms are often distorted in K-F-D's, as shown in K-F-D 7, where the brother's exceptionally long arm stealing cookies seems to be of some significance to 8-year-old Danny, who made the drawing.

Arm extensions may include cleaning implements (mops, brooms, vacuum cleaners, etc.), paint brushes (paddles?), weapons, and a host of other objects perceived as aids in controlling the environment.

COOKIES

BROTHER (4)
STEALING COOKIES

M

N

DAD
READING
SUNDAY
"TIMES"

M R (8)

TOBY (6 mos)
CRAWLING

∑ MOM

4

BEATING
ICING

BROTHER (7)
CLIMBING
LADDER
TO SLIDE

K-F-D 7

MASHING
UP FRUIT
(ME 8)

17

B. *Elevated Figures*

Throughout our K-F-D's, numerous techniques will be used to elevate various figures. Occasionally, a dominant sibling, for example, will be placed high above the rest of the figures. In children striving for dominance, one sees many techniques for placing their heads above the rest of the family figures. K-F-D 8 represents a very simple technique for elevating figures by placing them on boxes. It was done by 13-year-old Donna, who would like to be older, according to her statements and actions.

MOTHER

SELF
(13)

SISTER
(12)

BROTHER
(9)

C. Erasures

Erasures are often very significant in understanding some of the conflicts in our children. K-F-D 9, by 10-year-old Roger, reflects ambivalence. On the one hand, he would like to conform and grow up; on the other hand, he would like to be like his little brother, age 5. While Roger initially drew himself sitting next to the father in an identical grownup pose, he erased this and drew himself closer to the younger sibling in an identical position.

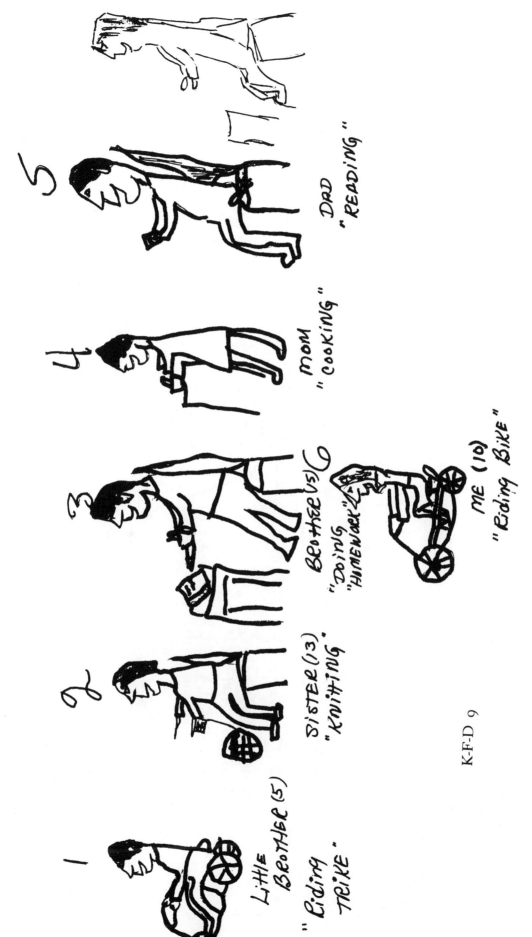

5

DAD
"READING"

4

MOM
"COOKING"

3

BROTHER(5)
"DOING
HOMEWORK"

ME (10)
"RIDING BIKE"

2

SISTER(13)
"KNITTING"

1

LITTLE
BROTHER (5)
"RIDING
TRIKE"

K-F-D 9

21

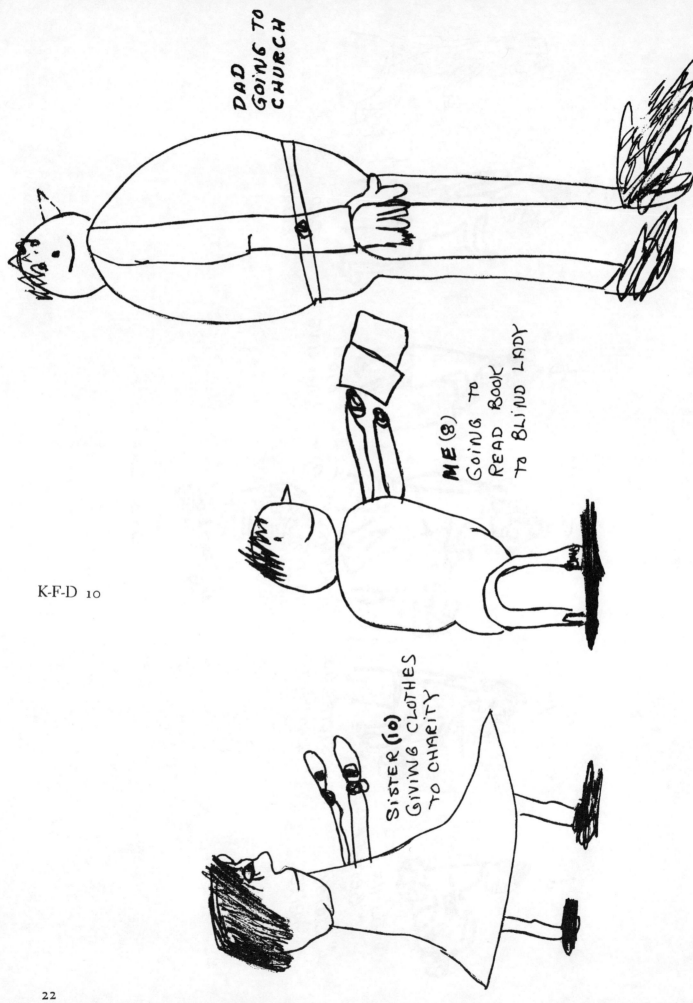

DAD
GOING TO
CHURCH

ME (8)
GOING TO
READ BOOK
TO BLIND LADY

SISTER (10)
GIVING CLOTHES
TO CHARITY

K-F-D 10

22

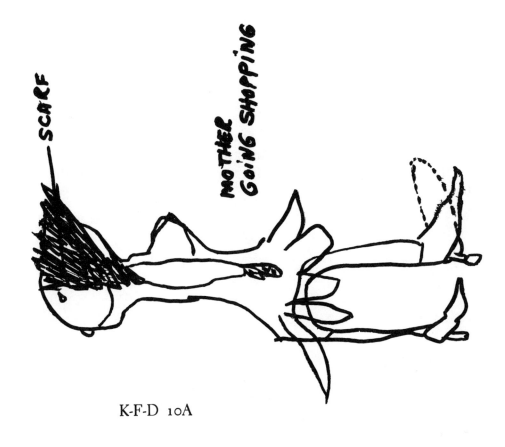

K-F-D 10A

D Figures on the Back of the Page

Many children will have difficulty with individual figures and will sit looking at the paper for prolonged periods. Some finally ask whether they can put the person on the back. K-F-D 10, by 8-year-old Bill, demonstrates such a drawing.

Billy had a great deal of conflict in relating to an overpowering, seductive mother. He refused to draw her with the family and placed her on the back of the paper. The figure he produced is shown in K-F-D 10A. The mother's figure is greatly distorted in comparison to the other three family members.

E. *Hanging*

Individual figures will often be seen in precarious positions. For example, 7-year-old Laura, who made K-F-D 11, shows herself on the edge of a roof. Even the car is in a precarious position and the father is falling. Hanging figures are usually associated with tension.

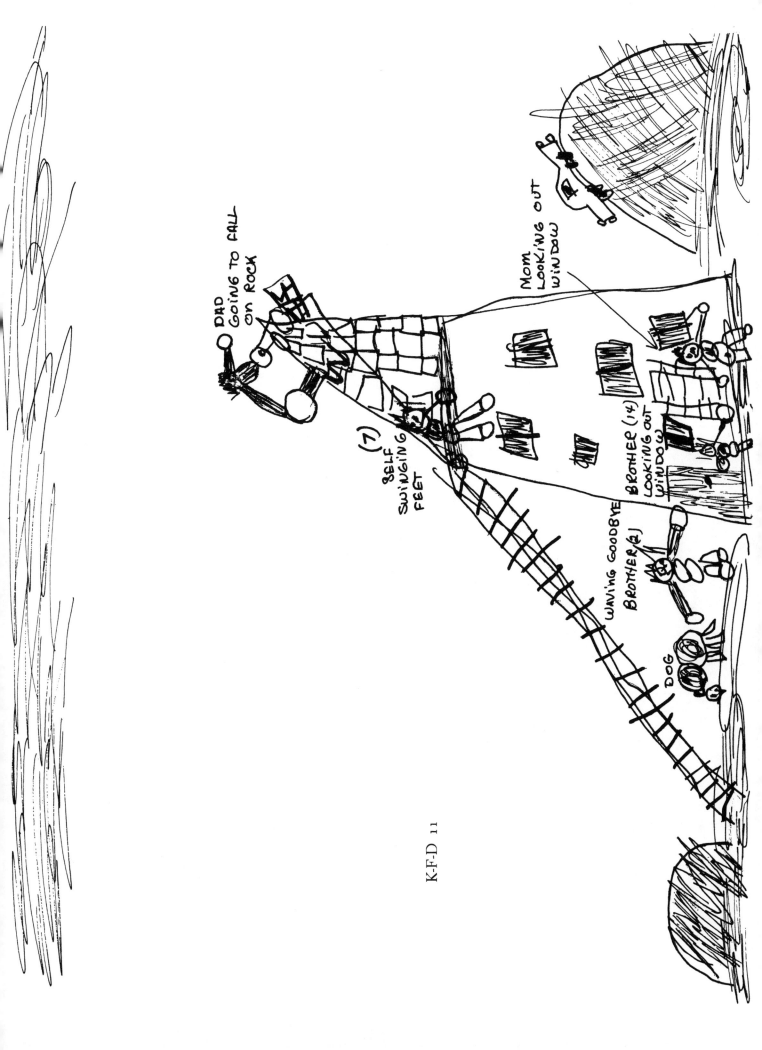

DAD
GOING TO FALL
ON ROCK

SELF
SWINGING
FEET
(7)

WAVING GOODBYE
BROTHER (2)

DOG

BROTHER (14)
LOOKING OUT
WINDOW

Mom
LOOKING OUT
WINDOW

K-F-D 11

K-F-D 12 shows a similar phenomenon, although we might call it leaning or falling. The father in this picture, done by 10-year-old Kevin, has been out of the family for a number of years and comes back occasionally. The dangerous position of the father and the great tension related to the boy's feelings about him is reflected in father "falling," which the boy then changed to "dancing."

Mother

me (10)

father

VACUUMING

PLAYING
GUITAR

"FALLING — No,
HE'S DANCING"

K-F-D 12

27

F. Omission of Body Parts

Often parts of an individual figure will be distorted or missing. There are numerous, very subtle ways of doing this. K-F-D 13, by 15-year-old Virginia, shows very obvious conflicts. She attempted heroically to reproduce a figure of herself, but she gave up, and even after prolonged urging could not draw herself.

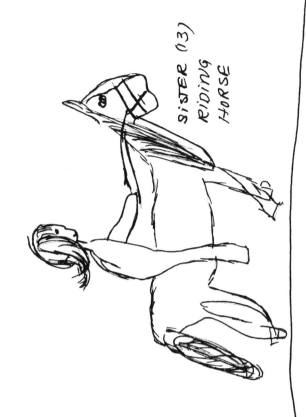

SISTER (13)
RIDING
HORSE

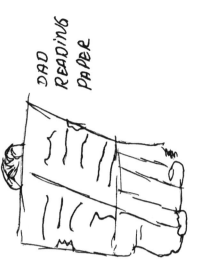

DAD
READING
PAPER

K-F-D 13

MA
STANDING

SELF (15)
(PASSED OUT)

G. Omission of Figures

Many examples can be found in our drawings of figures which cannot be drawn either on the front or the back of the paper. This frequently occurs when a new baby comes into the family, and the child refuses to draw him as a family member in the K-F-D.

H. Picasso Eye

K-F-D 14 was produced by 7-year-old Stephanie, brought in with symptoms of severe anxiety about her brother. The brother had been seriously ill with encephalitis some 1½ years prior to her referral. At the time of his illness, it was thought the boy would die, and there was great concern in the family about him. The Picasso eye, produced in the Self by Stephanie, reflects her concern and vigilance in relation to the brother: Stephanie is unable to compete with him and has much ambivalence and anger toward him which she cannot express.

I. *Rotated Figures*

In many of our drawings, there will be distortion in one of the figures in terms of its placement in relation to the other figures. Six-year-old Don, who did K-F-D 15, shows obvious distortion in rotating himself in relation to the other family members. This reflects his feelings of being different. Don demands *attention.*

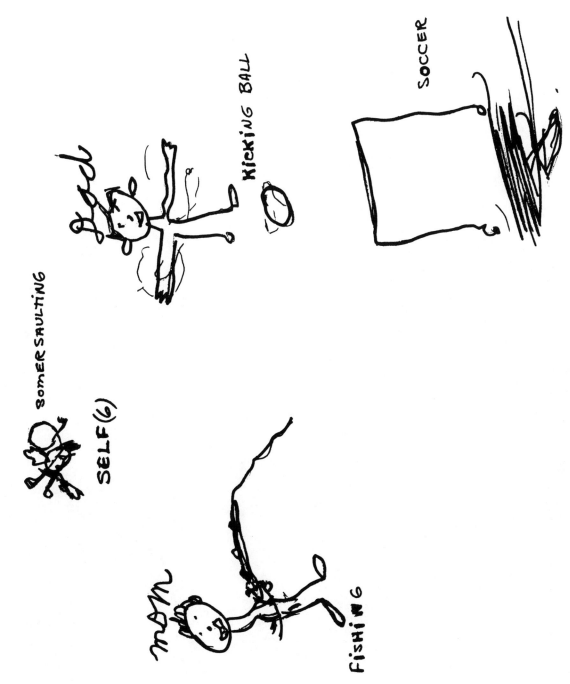

SOMERSAULTING

KICKING BALL

SOCCER

SELF (6)

FISHING

K-F-D 15

33

K-F-D 16 was done by 13-year-old Jim, recently placed in a new foster home. Jim felt different from the rest of the family, as suggested by his Self rotation.

These are some of the features of individual figures within the matrix of the K-F-D. The actions of and between the K-F-D figures are of primary concern in our next chapter.

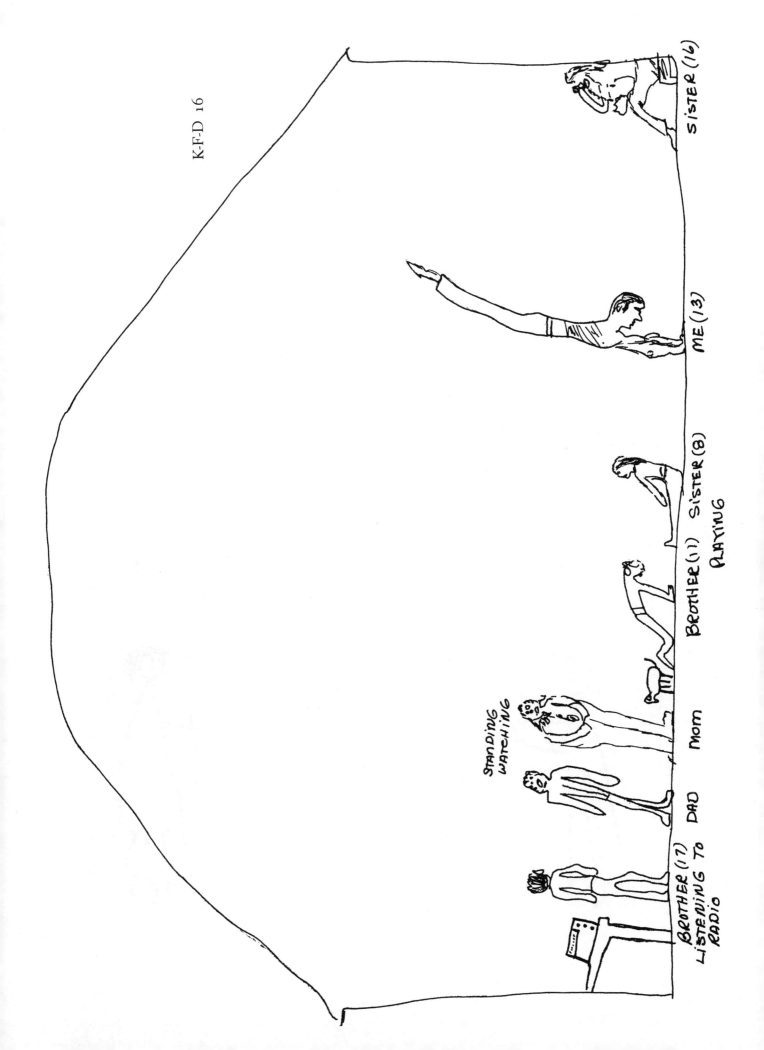

K-F-D 16

SISTER (16)

ME (13)

SISTER (8)
PLAYING

BROTHER (11)

Mom
STANDING
WATCHING

DAD

BROTHER (17)
LISTENING TO
RADIO

CHAPTER 4

K-F-D ACTIONS

INTRODUCTION

There is a movement of energy between people called by many names, such as, "interpersonal relations," "love," "libido," "valence," "feelings." This energy may vary in intensity from the low intensity of strangers . . .

STRANGERS

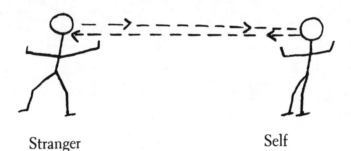

Stranger   Self

Fig 1—Strangers

. . . to the high intensity of ardent lovers.

LOVERS

Lover   Self

Fig. 2—Lovers

The energy may be condensed or symbolized in objects such as a ball.

COMPETITORS

Competitor   Self

Fig. 3—Competitors

Sometimes the energy is "fixated" or stationary, as when one wishes to compete with a handicapped sibling or a new baby but cannot.

NON-COMPETITORS

Handicapped Sibling   Self

Fig. 4—Non-Competitors

Sometimes energy is directed toward a taboo and approach-avoidance energies conflict.

CONFLICT

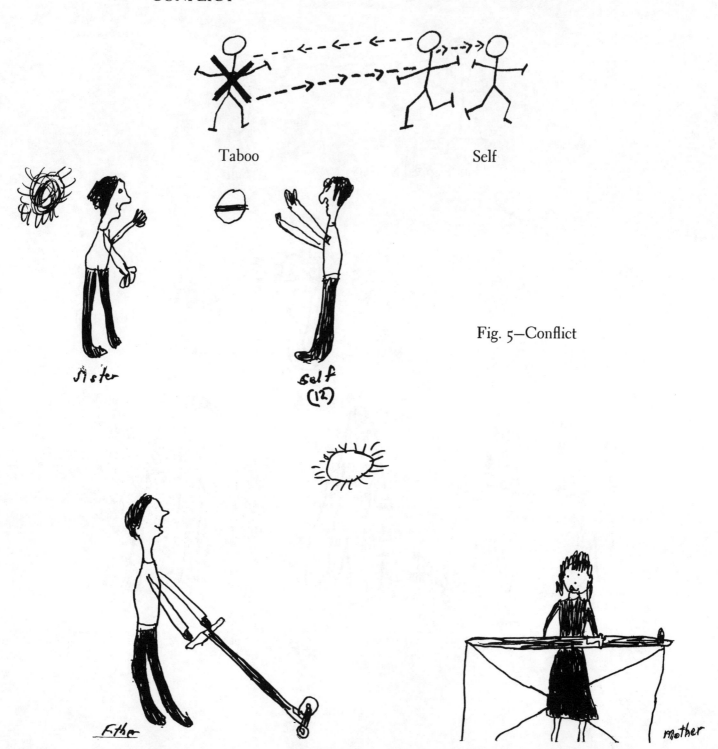

Taboo   Self

Fig. 5—Conflict

sister

self
(12)

Fther   mother

40

Energy may be "invested" or "internalized" in the Self during illness or threat.

ANXIETY

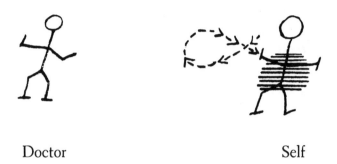

Doctor   Self

Fig. 6—Anxiety

Sometimes there are barriers erected to avoid this energy.

AVOIDANCE

Others   Self

Fig. 7—Avoidance

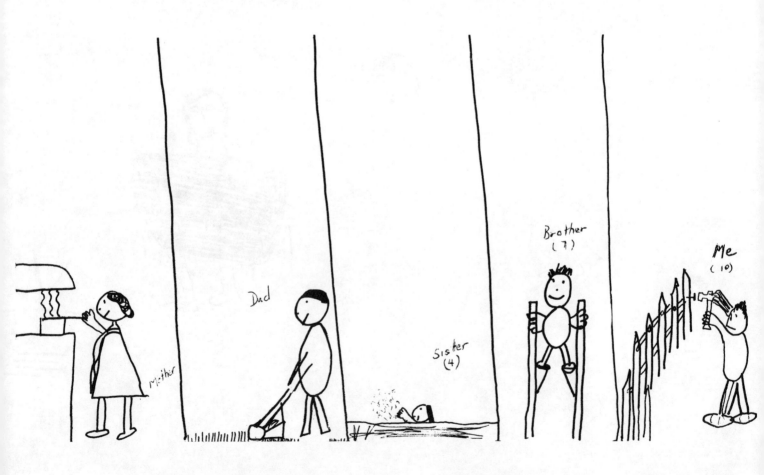

Sometimes love will overcome all barriers, conflicts and anxieties.

HARMONY

Harmony

Fig. 8—Harmony

In this chapter, we see the movement or energy reflected in the various K-F-D actions as children depict their "interpersonal relations" within the family constellation.

A. AGE and SEX

The age and sex of the children who did the K-F-D's are shown in Table 1. The frequency of the K-F-D variables found in this book (with the exception of the normal K-F-D's) have been combined with those from the introductory K-F-D book (5) to produce Tables 1, 3, 4, 5 and 6. As can be seen, the Mean Age for both boys and girls is about 10, with a range from 5 to 20 and skewed toward the 10 and below age group.

Age	Male	Female
5	2	2
6	5	1
7	12	9
8	24	8
9	12	10
10	24	9
11	13	6
12	10	6
13	10	4
14	8	1
15	1	5
16	4	2
17	3	
18		1
19		
20		1
$\bar{x}=10.14$	----	----
$\bar{x}=10.33$	N=128	N=65

Table No. 1—Age and Sex

It may be noted that the boys outnumber the girls about 2 to 1. This ratio is representative of that found by many clinics treating disturbed children.

B. ACTIONS OF INDIVIDUAL K-F-D FIGURES

A list of the most common actions of individual K-F-D figures is shown in Table No. 2.

Babysitting	Fishing	Picking Up	Spraying
Batting	Flying	Planting	Standing
Being Hurt	Grooming	Playing Alone	Sun Bathing
Burning	Hammering	Playing Music	Sweeping
Catching	Hanging	Playing with Someone	Swimming
Cleaning	Helping	Raking	Swinging
Climbing	Hiding	Reading	Talking
Coloring	Hitting	Repairing	Telephoning
Cooking	Hosing	Riding	Throwing
Crawling	Hurting	Rivaling	Vacuuming
Crying	Ironing	Running	Waiting
Cutting	Jumping	Sailing	Walking
Digging	Kicking	Schoolwork (doing)	Washing Clothes
Drawing	Kite Flying	Sewing	Washing Dishes
Dressing	Knitting	Shooting	Washing the Car
Driving	Listening	Shopping	Watching
Drying	Looking	Shouting	Watching TV
Eating	Lying in Bed	Sitting	Waving
Falling	Making Beds	Skiing	Whistling
Feeding Animals	Mowing	Skin Diving	Working
Feeding People	Ordering	Sleeping	Writing (typewriting)
Fighting	Painting	Smoking	

Table No. 2—Common Actions of Individual K-F-D Figures

FREQUENCY OF ACTIONS

1. *Father*—The most frequent actions of the father as shown by girls and boys are found in Table No. 3.

Girls (57)		Boys (120)	
Reading	7%	Mowing	8%
Cooking	5%	Cutting	8%
Working	5%	Reading	6%
Burning	4%	Repairing	5%
Mowing	4%	Painting	5%
Helping	4%	Watching TV	5%
		Working	5%

Table No. 3—Father's Actions

45

2. *Mother*—The most frequent actions of the mother as shown by girls and boys are found in Table 4.

Girls (64)		Boys (124)	
Cooking	14%	Cooking	16%
Washing dishes	8%	Helping	6%
Making beds	6%	Ironing	6%
Playing with	5%	Planting	5%
Vacuuming	5%	Vacuuming	5%
		Sweeping	4%
		Washing dishes	4%
		Sewing	4%

Table No. 4—Mother's Actions

3. *Self*—The most frequent actions of the Self as shown by girls and boys are found in Table No. 5.

Girls (65)		Boys (128)	
Playing	6%	Playing	13%
Eating	6%	Eating	6%
Walking	6%	Throwing	5%
Riding	5%	Riding	5%
Dishwashing	5%	Watching TV	5%

Table No. 5—Self Actions

C. ACTION BETWEEN K-F-D FIGURES

Many of our drawings will reflect a "field of force" within the picture or between the figures. These forces may be conceptualized in a number of ways. Kurt Lewin (18) might have discussed the drawings in terms of positive and negative valences and various barriers. Freud's (11) concept of libido, a form of energy, at times invested in a particular person or part of the environment might also be a way to describe the forces depicted in the K-F-D's. Behaviorists, such as B. F. Skinner (24), might call the emphasized parts of the drawings "discriminative stimuli."

1. BALLS—Most frequently in our drawings, the force will take the form of a ball. For example, in K-F-D 17, by 10-year-old Marvin, the football sailing between the brother and the father may be interpreted as a force between the two. Marvin also has energies depicted by the ball above his head, but these seem not to be directed. It is noted that he compartmentalizes the drawing and tends to identify with the girls in the family.

46

K-F-D 17

Mom

ME (10)

SISTER (11)

DAD

BROTHER (7)

SISTER (5)

1. BALLS (Cont.)

In K-F-D 18, we have 8-year-old Ronald, who has a great rivalry with his older brother. However, the brother is much "above" him and does not compete with him on a level the 8-year-old would desire. He is afraid to compete with the cutting father. Placing the mother and the baby in the house is a way to encapsulate them and perhaps to separate Ronald from his father.

Dad mowing

Baby (1½) in pen

Mom "doing dishes"

Me (8) throwing football

football

BROTHER (11) Climbing tree

K-F-D 18

49

1. BALLS (Cont.)

K-F-D 19 was done by 11½-year-old George, who had an extremely threatening and punishing father figure. He finds it impossible to compete with such a figure. We see the pathetic size of the ball (force) and the inability to direct the force toward the father. In contrast, the sister is able to interact with the mother and is "kicking" the football. This is the drawing of a boy who has a regressive reaction to an extremely threatening father. While he has basic competitive feelings, he does not dare "throw the ball."

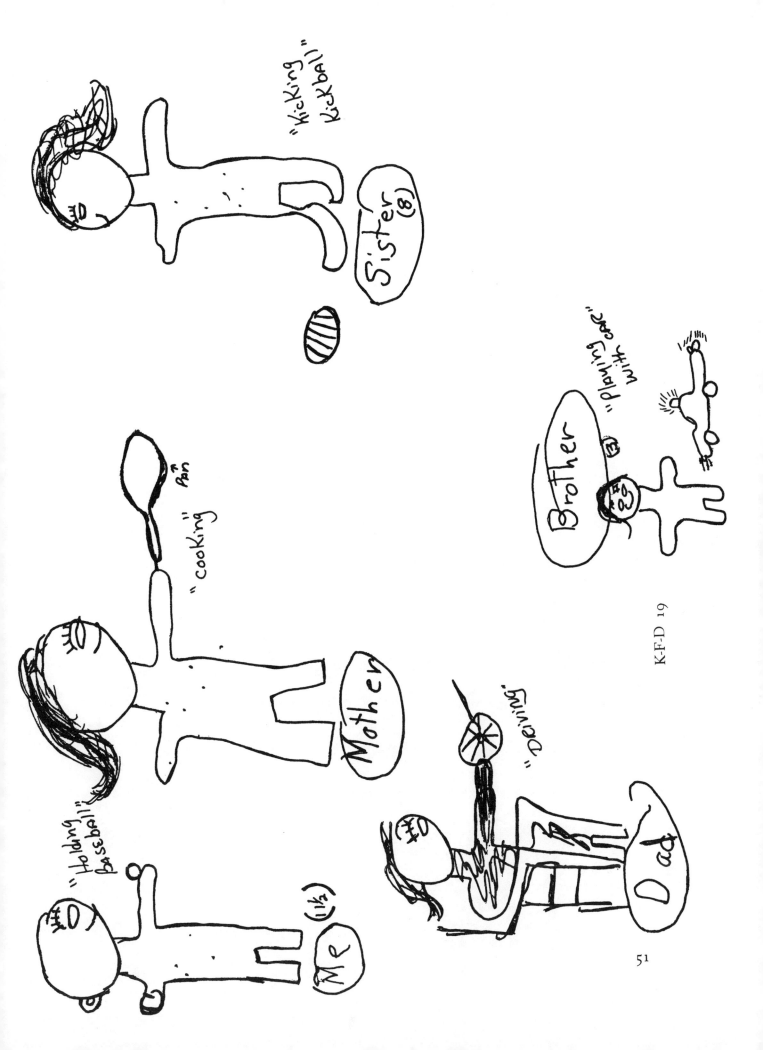

"Kicking Kickball"

Sister (8)

"Playing care with"

Brother

"cooking" Pan

Mother

"Deiving"

Dad

"Holding Baseball"

Me (11½)

K-F-D 19

51

1. BALLS (Cont.)

K-F-D 20, by 8-year-old Billy, also reflects an inability to compete with a threatening father figure. However, Billy is extremely competitive outside the family, and the size of the ball, which is aloft but not directed toward the father, reflects his desire to compete.

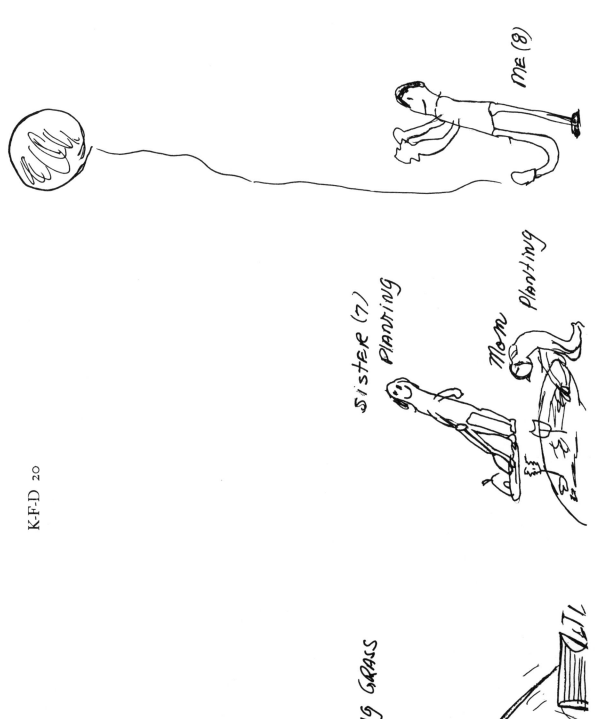

ME (8)

Sister (7) Planting

Mom Planting

Dad Cutting Grass

53

1. BALLS (Cont.)

Often competition or jealousy is depicted by the path of the ball. For example, K-F-D 21, by 8-year-old Heather, shows her interacting with the mother through the medium of the ball. However, there is no interaction between the girl and the younger sister, and she and the mother are depicted as playing "Keep-away from June."

Keep away from June

Playing ball game

me (8)

mom

June (5)

1. BALLS (Cont.)

K-F-D 22 is that of an extremely competitive 10-year-old girl. In drawing the picture, Charlene first made an extremely large ball, which she erased and then reduced in size. She is pitching to the brother, who is recipient of the action. The 4-year-old brother, who has been ill, is shaded and encapsulated in the middle of the drawing, isolated from any competition suggested in the force and size of the ball.

Mom
" picking out a
dress from
store "

Dad
" watching
TV "

Sister
(11)
Combing
hair

Brother (4)
" in bed "

Brother (5)
" batting "

ME (10)
" playing ball "

K-F-D 22

1. BALLS (Cont.)

In K-F-D 23, we see competitive 12½-year-old George with a severe "sawing" father. This father puts a great deal of emphasis on school achievement, and perhaps the "A"'s serving as the saw-horses show George's feelings about the ascendent father's concern with his poor school performance. George is directing the ball (force) in the father's direction, but he does not dare aim it directly at him.

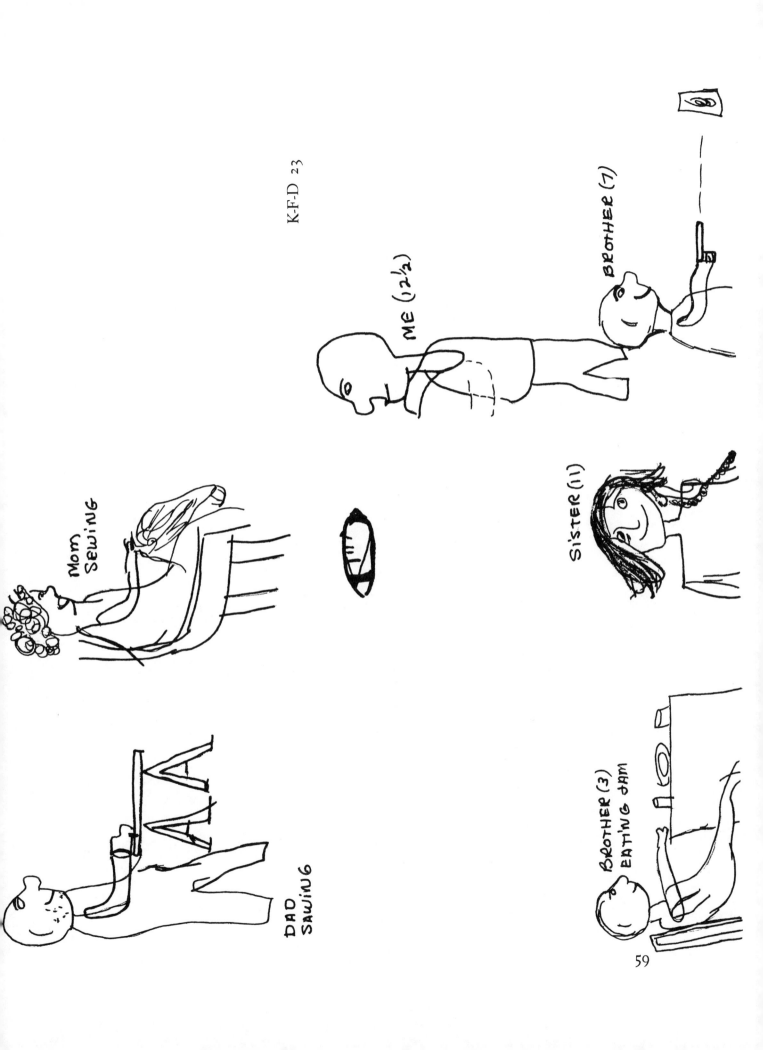

K-F-D 23

Mom SEWING

DAD SAWING

ME (12½)

BROTHER (7)

SISTER (11)

BROTHER (3) EATING JAM

59

1. BALLS (Cont.)

K-F-D 24 was made by 8-year-old Martha, who is extremely competitive. However, while she would like to compete with the mother for the father's affections, she is unable to do so. The stove serves as a barrier and the force of the ball is directed toward the ground. This is a little girl who, outside the family, always wants to be the leader, but within the family she finds it difficult to compete with her mother and older sister.

K-F-D 24

Dad writing at desk

Mom cooking

playing ball
me (8)

sister (13)
walking on phone

61

1. BALLS (Cont.)

K-F-D 25 is by 8½-year-old Ann, who is in competition with her younger brother. However, he has been quite ill, and she cannot compete with him, although she is tied to him through the action of pulling the wagon. The ball, however, is close to him and the energies are immobilized and perhaps "fixated" or "invested in" the brother. Note the shaded areas, i.e., under the brother, the ball, and the mother's hands. This suggests that the energies (angers?) directed toward the brother are inhibited by Mother's hands.

1. BALLS (Cont.)

K-F-D 26 was produced by 12-year-old Jack, described as a "loner." He is competitive but is unable to compete with his overwhelming parents. Jack has the ball (energy) going around in a circular fashion in the tetherball game. The energy is thus not directed toward any figure, but he tends to keep it to himself and is bound up by his inability to direct it toward the environment.

The circular movement of Jack's tetherball and the circular "pool" in which the father fishes may well be related in fantasy. The preoccupation with circular movement is associated with schizoid personalities.

Dad
FISHING

Mom
iRONING

TETHER BALL

ME (IR)

K-F-D 26

65

1a. BALL BOUNCING—Frequently, for various reasons, children who desire to compete will be unable to do so. K-F-D 27, made by 9-year-old Tom, reflects this inability to direct the force of his competition. He has two extremely threatening parents— a castrating father and an over-meticulous, compulsive mother. He dares not direct this competitiveness toward any member of the family; thus, he stands rather helplessly "bouncing the ball up and down."

1a. BALL BOUNCING (Cont.)

This theme is repeated in K-F-D 28, produced by 8-year-old David, an extremely competitive boy, who places himself high above the other members of the family. But, because of a threatening father (compartmentalized and "watching fights"), David dares not compete directly and is "throwing the ball in the ground."

K-F-D 28

When David was asked to "Draw a Person," he did D-A-P 28A. Note the size of the drawing and the flared nostrils, suggesting anger. The assertive, aggressive features of David's D-A-P are not suggested in the immature K-F-D Self except in the placement "above" the other family members and the force of the ball.

D-A-P 28A

1b. BALL-ON-THE-HEAD—In K-F-D 29, we see 14-year-old Lee, who is very jealous of his 10-month-old brother. He feels rejected by the parents, as suggested by their turning their faces from him. He wants to compete with the baby but doesn't know how, so at times he identifies with him and regresses, but he cannot interact with him in "the ball game." Lee is the oldest of five brothers. He compartmentalized the family, showing his desire to be close to the parents. His feeling of rejection is depicted by their turning away from him. Lee would like to direct action (the ball) toward the baby but is unable to do so.

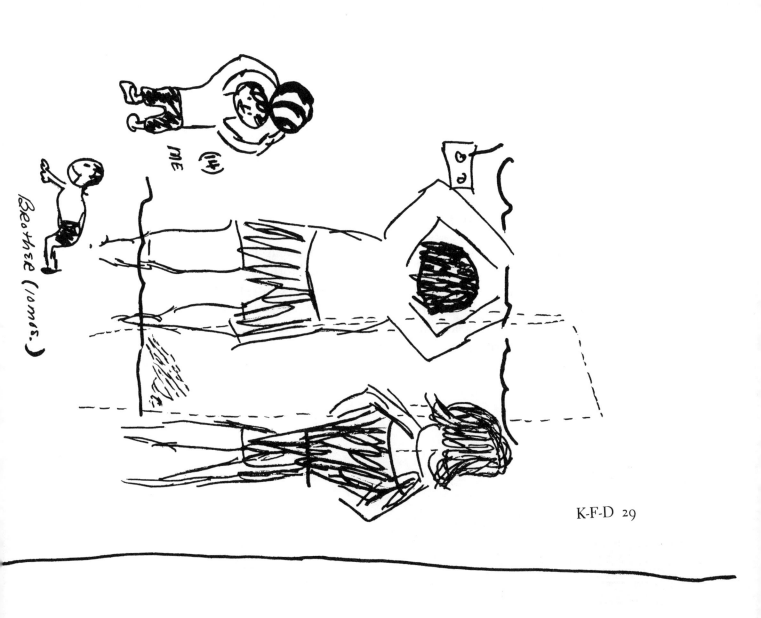

ME (14)

Brother (10 mos.)

K-F-D 29

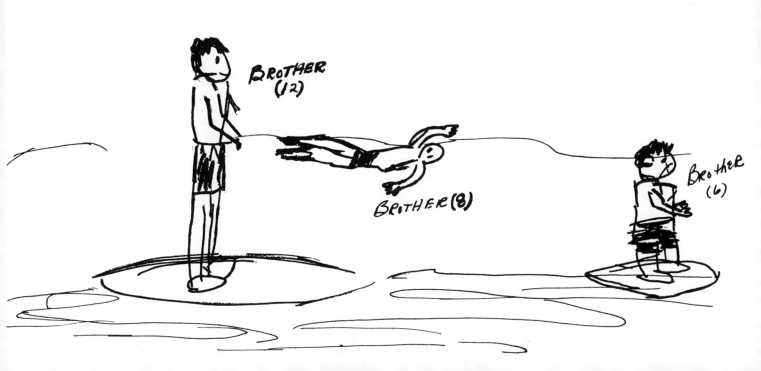

BROTHER (12)

BROTHER (8)

BROTHER (6)

1b. BALL-ON-THE-HEAD (Cont.)

K-F-D 30 is by 8-year-old Todd, whose 6-year-old brother is retarded. Thus, the competition between the brothers is inhibited. While Todd is very competitive, he directs his competition away from the brother by kicking the ball. The retarded brother has a large "ball-on-the-head" suggesting Todd's desire to direct action toward the brother but inability to do so.

MOM

"WATCHING TV"

Dad

EATING CHICKEN

brother (6)

"BALL

me (8)

KicKin'
BALL

73

1b. BALL-ON-THE-HEAD (Cont.)

In K-F-D 31, we perhaps see more clearly the inability to compete with an overwhelming younger sibling. In this family, the 3-year-old brother is the "center of attention" and very close to the father, who is very protective of him. The tremendous energy invested in the figure of the younger brother is shown by the four balls on top of his head. Ten-year-old Phillip escapes from this competition by soaring with his kite to the level of his dominant 15-year-old "cutting" brother. It would seem that much of Phillip's energy is "tied up" with the younger brother.

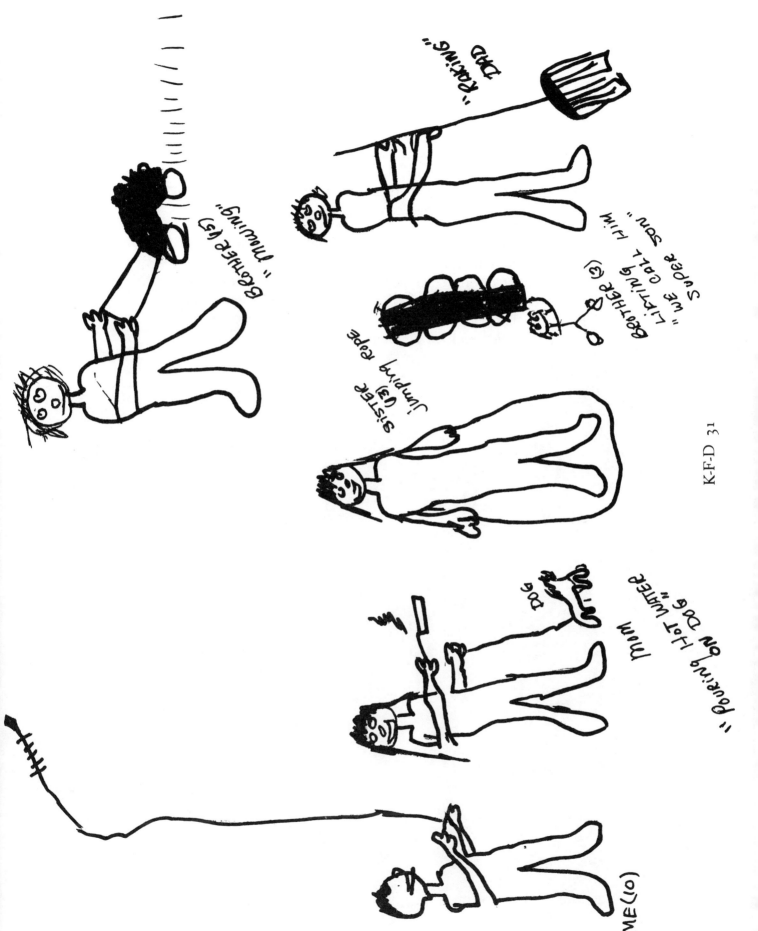

"RAKING"
DAD

BROTHER (3)
LIFTING HIM
"WE CALL HIM
SUPER SON"

BROTHER (5)
"MOWING"

SISTER (3)
JUMPING ROPE

K-F-D 31

MOM
"POURING HOT DOG"
DOG

ME (10)

75

2. BARRIERS—Examples of barriers to action in the drawings are so pervasive and so varied that no specific examples are given. In many of the drawings, barriers are subtly formed by placing objects, walls or lines between figures.

3. DANGEROUS OBJECTS—Throughout our drawings, we see objects such as balls directed at other figures. Occasionally the anger associated with such direction is more obvious. For example, in K-F-D 32, Dad is described as "ready to pound something." From the direction, one suspects that if the action were to continue, it would result in a pounding of 10-year-old Greg, who produced the drawing.

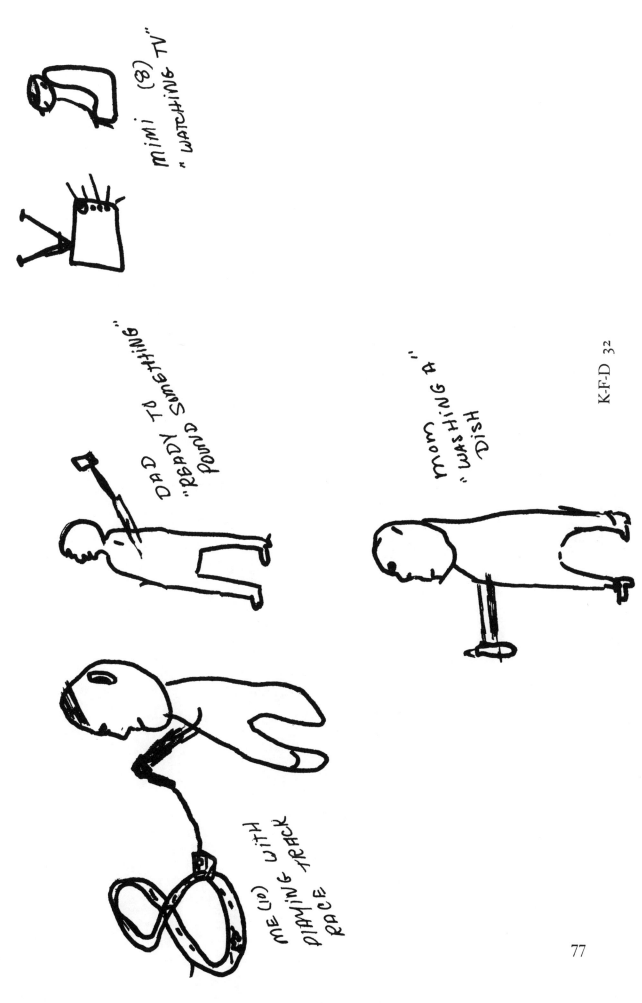

mimi (8)
"WATCHING TV"

DAD TO
"READY SOMETHING
POUND"

MOM (40)
"WASHING A
DISH"

ME (10) WITH
PLAYING TRACK
RACE

K-F-D 32

77

4. HEAT, LIGHT, WARMTH

4a. FIRE—While the fire theme often combines anger and the need for warmth (love), sometimes the latter is obvious. K-F-D 33, by 10-year-old Barbara, depicts the favored brother, Paul, 9, sitting next to the father, absorbing the warmth from the fire. At this stage of her development, Barbara is very much in competition for the father's love. She places the mother upside down and separates the rest of the family from Father. However, she cannot separate the father from his favorite son, so she shows the light from the TV shining upon her and shares some of the warmth from the fire, but at a distance.

MOTHER
COOKING

BROTHER
(17)
WATCHING
MOTHER
COOK

Kitchen

MIKE
(16)

playing cards

PETER
(15)

ME (10)
WATCHING
TV

Living room

BROTHER (9)
SITTING BY
FIRE

FATHER
READING PAPER

K-F-D 33

4a. FIRE (Cont.)

K-F-D 34 depicts young Annie, who is very angry with her mother because of her attention to baby sister. Annie shows Mother serving food, but her anger with Mother carries over to the smoke and heat coming from the popcorn. She seems to bar the mother from access to the baby sister by her outstretched arms, suggesting also Annie's need for power. She is standing on a stool to elevate herself, and the extension of the trunk also suggests need to be more important and higher. This is a very striving little girl who is "burning mad" at the mother, and who is actively trying to distract the mother's attention from the baby.

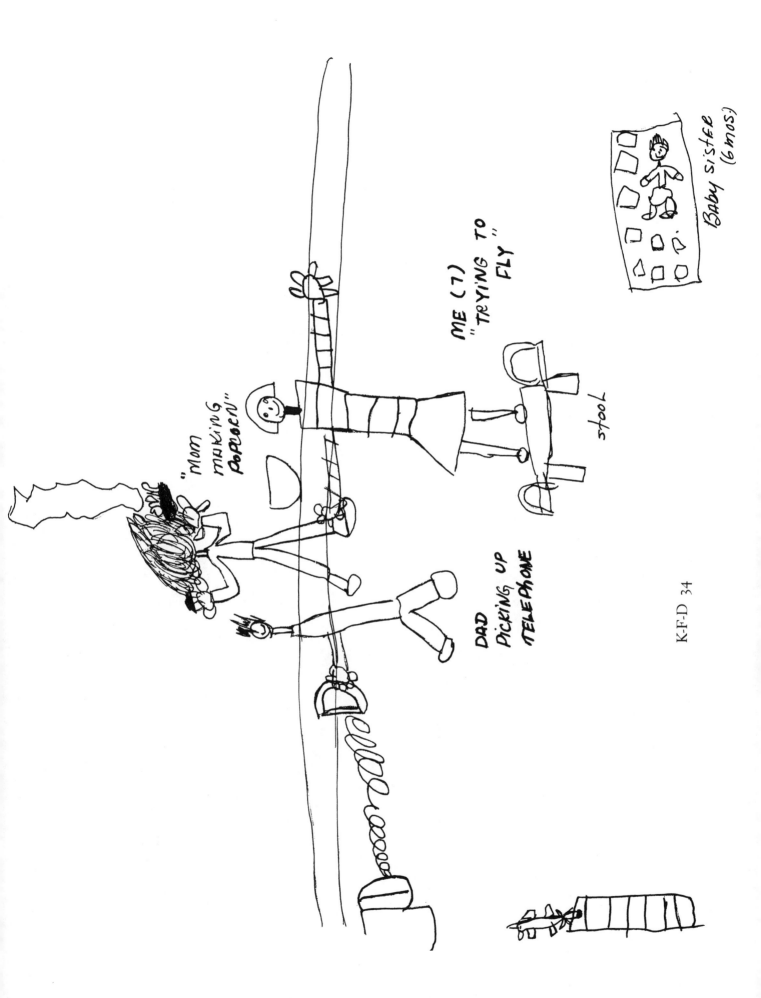

"Mom making POPCORN"

ME (7) "TRYING TO FLY"

DAD PICKING UP TELEPHONE

stool

Baby sister (6 mos.)

K-F-D 34

4b. LIGHTS—The lights in our drawings are commonly drawn by children with a need for love. K-F-D 35, by young David, who is very unsure of his mother's love, is completely dominated by the light (love). The baby brother is encapsulated and directly below the light, while David huddles very close to his mother in an attempt to get her warmth, although Mother is still facing the baby.

K-F-D 35

EATING

ME (7)

MOM

DAD

SISTER (9)

SISTER (13)

BABY BROTHER (5 MOS)

SISTER (5)

83

4b. LIGHTS (Cont.)

The light theme is repeated in K-F-D 36, done by 8½-year-old Billy, who had a history of deprivation. The parents were divorced, and the boy had lived with several relatives. One notes that while he is reaching for the food on the table, it is very difficult for him to touch it. The light above him reflects his need for warmth and love.

KF-D 36

MINDY (10) WALKING TO TABLE

MOM EATING

ME (8½) EATING

Brother (6) EATING

4b. LIGHTS (Cont.)

In K-F-D 37, we see somewhat different dynamics. Tim, an 8½-year-old boy, had lived with his mother following her separation from her first husband. Mother and son were very close and the boy had been sleeping with her for a number of years. Mother had recently remarried. Note the lights above the mother and Tim, and the stepfather carrying the firewood. The need to compete for the mother's love is suggested by the lights above the son and mother, but not above the stepfather.

KFD 37

4b. LIGHTS (Cont.)

K-F-D 38 depicts some other reasons for the dominance of the light. In the drawing, the family is encapsulated under the light. It is a regressed drawing. The whole family is helping mother. The father had been killed a year-and-a-half earlier in an accident. John, 7½ years old, came in with a history of soiling and extremely regressive behavior. The mother had not yet recovered from the loss of the loved father, nor had the boy. The great need for warmth and love in this family is suggested by the dominant symbol of the light.

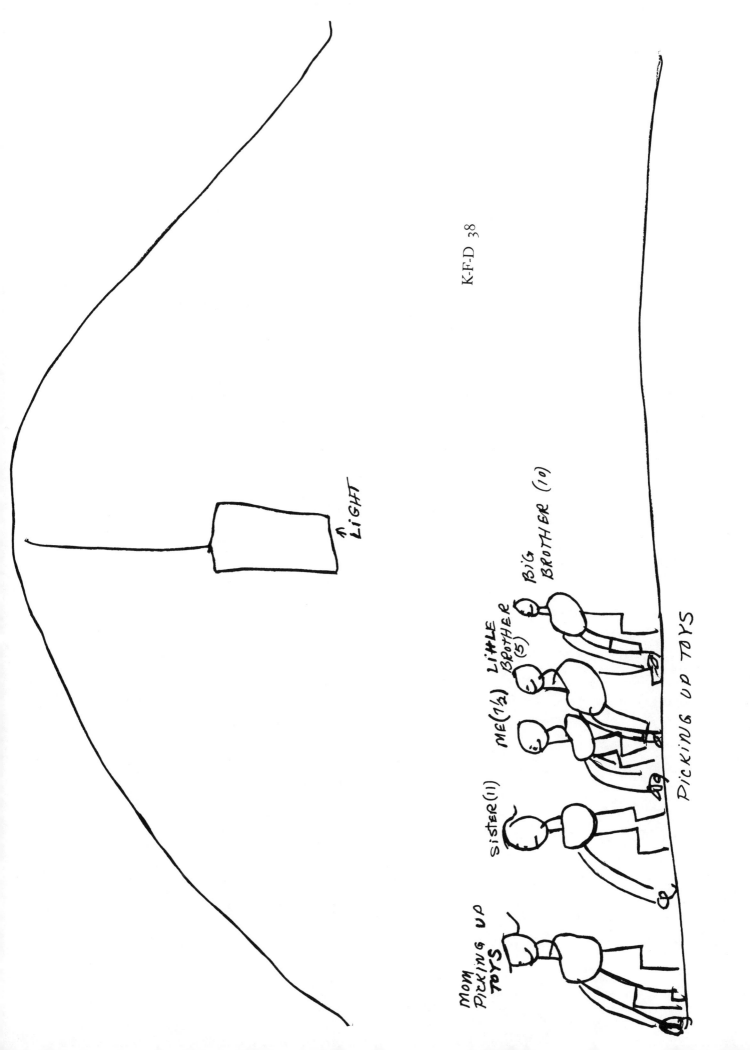

LIGHT

K-F-D 38

MOM
PICKING UP
TOYS

SISTER (11)

ME (7½)

LITTLE
BROTHER
(5)

BIG
BROTHER (10)

PICKING UP TOYS

4b. LIGHTS (Cont.)

K-F-D 39, produced by a gifted boy, age 7, depicts a very imaginative and symbolic handling of the light theme. Alfred has need to be ascendent and he is, indeed, the center of the drawing and far above the others. However, he is inside the light and is swinging over to the sun for more warmth. The light and heat dominate his world. It is noted that there is an 11-year-old mentally retarded brother and a 3-year-old sister with extreme learning problems. The parents have been preoccupied in meeting the needs of the retarded children, and Alfred resents this; he has great need to be loved. The usual Oedipal theme of competing with the father for the mother's affection at this age is also seen. It is noted that he has a direct line down to the mother. She is said to be very angry with the father because "he might break the light." This drawing symbolically reflects a great struggle to be loved by a gifted, competitive boy.

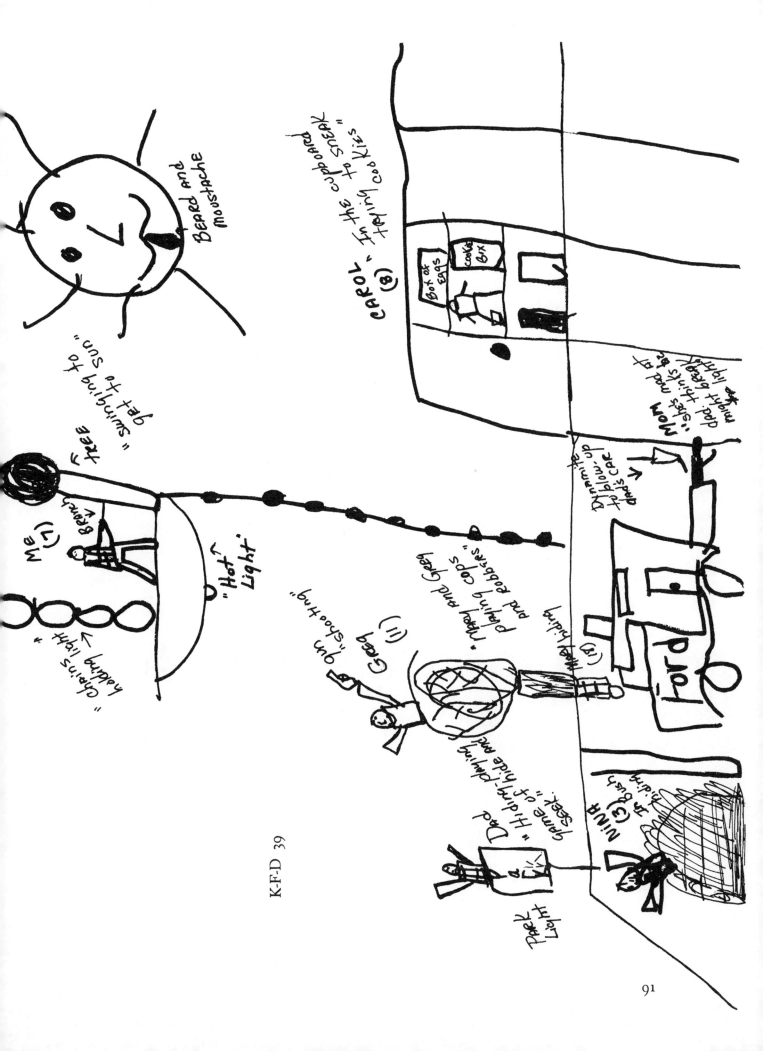

Beard and Moustache

CAROL (8) - In the cupboard trying to sneak

"Swinging to get light at sun"

FREE

Branch

ME (7)

"Hot Light"

"Chains light burglary"

gun "shooting"

Greg (11)

"Mom and Greg playing and good robbers cops"

Dad "Hiding-playing and seek" Game of Hide and

Park Light

NINA (3) Bush hiding

Dynamite to blow-up dad's car

Mom "She's mad to think pop-shirts might light"

running light

Ford

K-F-D 39

4b. LIGHTS (Cont.)

K-F-D 40, by 13-year-old Harvey, shows overwhelming force in the drawing of the light. Harvey has been sent away to boarding school because of behavioral problems. He feels quite isolated from the rest of the family, as depicted by the barriers between him and the parents. In his relative isolation, Harvey feels that the two younger children in the family get all of the love; indeed, the light is shining down on them and will have a difficult time penetrating Harvey's own self-imposed barrier.

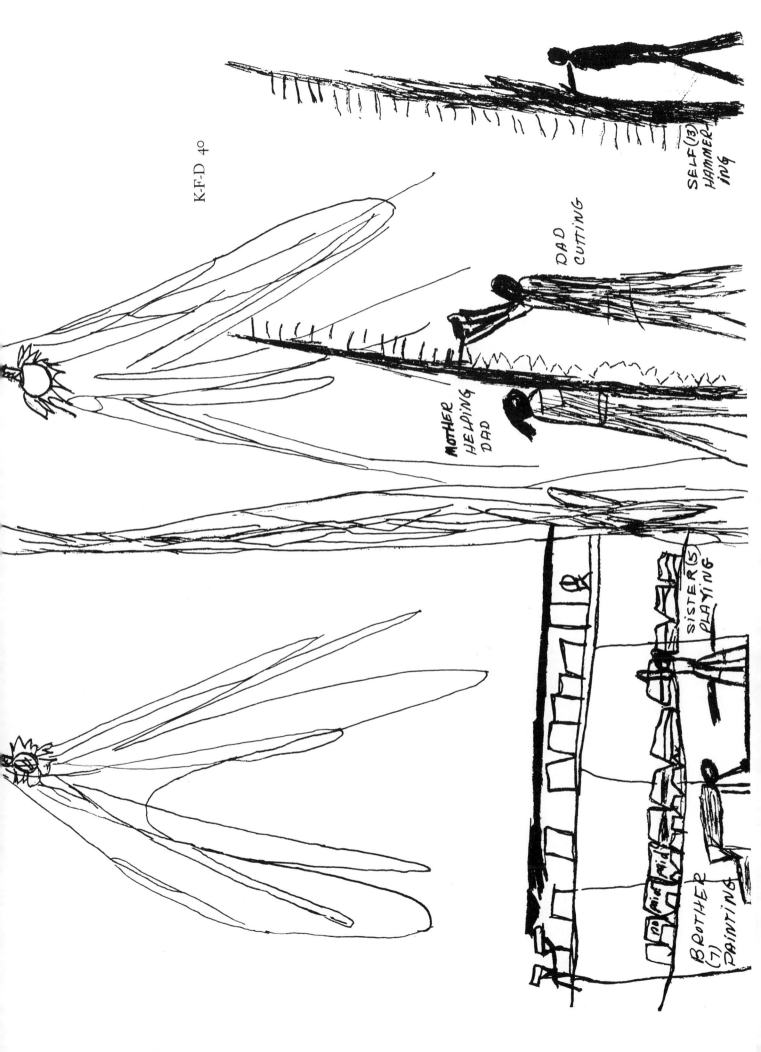

K-F-D 40

SELF (13) HAMMER-ING

DAD CUTTING

MOTHER HELPING DAD

SISTER (5) PLAYING

BROTHER (7) PAINTING

4b. LIGHTS (Cont.)

In K-F-D 41, by 13-year-old Steve, we see a disintegrated personality. This boy feels inadequate, as reflected by his tiny Self drawing. The distortions in the figures are obvious. This is a schizoid type of adjustment which is close to real schizophrenia. Note, however, that the central theme of the drawing is a light. At this time, however, the bugs are on the light, symbolizing Steve's obsessive need for warmth. Steve is literally "bugged" by his striving for light (love). He is having difficulty defining reality, but a central theme of need for warmth and love is reflected in the heavily darkened central light and perhaps the equally heavily shaded mother.

BUGS ON A LIGHT

FATHER TURNING out LIGHT

MODEL AIRPLANE

ME (13)

← CHAIR

HAND

MA BUYING SKI GLOVES

BROTHER (15) HAVING BLOOD TESTED

K-F-D 41

95

4c. ELECTRICITY—Many children with great need for warmth and love and also power have some distortion in their thoughts, often reflected in their preoccupation with electricity. Perhaps this is best illustrated in a series of drawings by 11½-year-old Tim. In Tim's D-A-P, 42A, the distortions in the shoulder and neck area and the accentuated shoulders suggest a need for power.

Then asked to produce a Kinetic Family Drawing, he started it as shown in K-F-D 42B. One sees in the drawing the passing of electricity through the mother. Tim is obviously in control of the heat and power directed toward his mother. Tim was, however, extremely threatened by the drawing, refused to continue and insisted on starting again.

Tim's complete K-F-D is shown in K-F-D 42. He is still playing with electricity, but he is distant from the mother, who is separated by compartmentalization. He is sitting in the same position as the father, who seems to be serving as the boy's control. One notes the extreme barrier of the wall between the boy and his sister and the perhaps displaced wall near the younger sister.

One saw initially in the possibly less guarded K-F-D 42B the association the boy has with the electricity controlling and even passing through the mother. This electrical theme will be repeated in the K-F-D's and can be seen in many subtle forms.

D-A-P 42A

K-F-D 42B

96

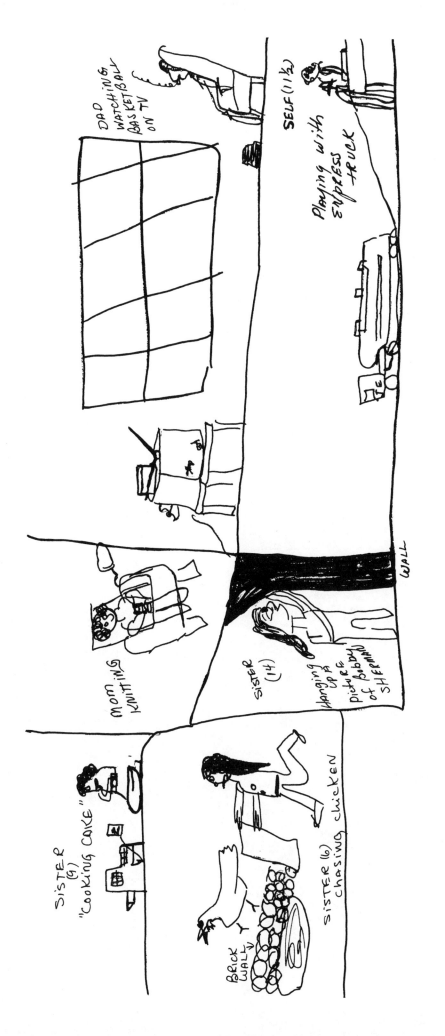

DAD WATCHING BASKETBALL ON TV

SELF (11½)

Playing with express truck

MOM KNITTING

SISTER (14)

Hanging up a picture of Bobby of SHERMAN

WALL

SISTER (9) "COOKING CAKE"

SISTER (6) chasing chicken

BRICK WALL

K-F-D 42

97

4c. ELECTRICITY (Cont.)

K-F-D 43 was done by 12½-year-old Bill, who was referred because of his obsessive preoccupation with electricity. He was described as an isolate who had significant problems of sexual activity and masturbation. One sees the connection between the electricity and the sexual theme in his interest in the fuse box with the phallic-like symbol of repair.

our family

MUMMY PAINTING

dad LOOKING AT ROCKS

SISTER (11) SITTING DOWN CHANGING SISTER

SISTER (2)

BROTHER (8) PLAYING BASEBALL

SISTER (6) READING

ME (12½) SCREWING in SCREW for fuse box.

4c. ELECTRICITY (Cont.)

K-F-D 44, by 8-year-old Gordon, reflects the need for power and control in a highly striving young male. The electrical waves give him control over the ironing mother.

SELF (8)

MOTHER IRONING

K-F-D 44

FATHER
TESTING ROCKETS

4d. IRONING AND SUNSHINE—K-F-D 45 was produced by 5½-year-old Ted, brought in because his mother had recurrent thoughts of destroying him. Ted was conceived out of wedlock, and his mother was ambivalent in her struggle to accept him. It is noted that the sun (warmth) completely bathes the father and brother. Ted is connected to the mother, who is ironing—perhaps the warmest K-F-D maternal activity. It is noted, however, that Ted is digging a ditch. The theme of getting dirty or digging dirt is seen in the drawings of children who associate "dirty" and "bad." The intensity of Ted's struggle to obtain love (warmth), though Mother feels he is "bad (dirty)," is vividly depicted in this drawing.

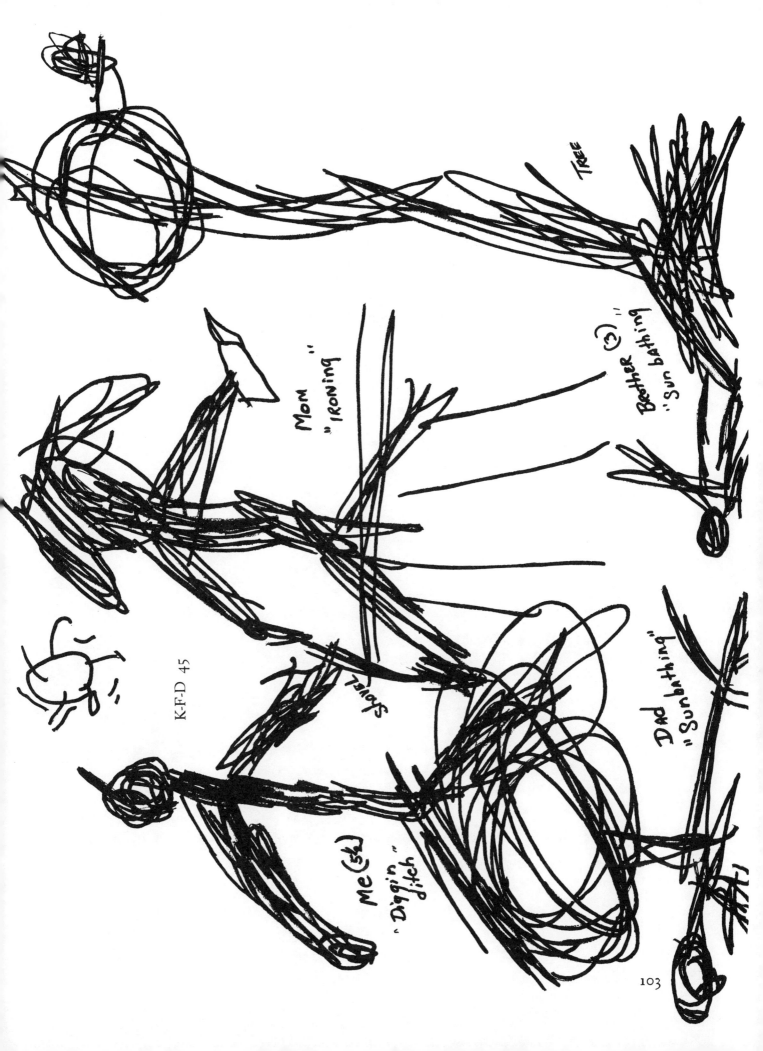

TREE

Brother
"Sun bathing" (3)

Mom
"Ironing"

K-F-D 45

Shovel

Me (5th)
"Diggin'
ditch"

Dad
"Sunbathing"

103

4d. IRONING AND SUNSHINE (Cont.)

In some families the affection or need for warmth is displaced from the mother to an older sister. In K-F-D 46, by 8-year-old Bobby, we see him very close to his sister and isolated from the rest of the family through compartmentalization. Mother is missing, but warm Sister, who is ironing, has taken her place.

4d. IRONING AND SUNSHINE (Cont.)

In more pathological forms we see some children who have great need for warmth, but some have an extremely strong conscience. Warren, 8 years old, produced K-F-D 47. One notes not only the compartmentalization but also the rotation and isolation of his figure from the rest of the family. The extremely threatening family figures with their distortion—the sister actually pushing him away with a very long arm and the piercing eye of the father —are associated with the ironing mother and the boy's great conflict in desiring his mother's love.

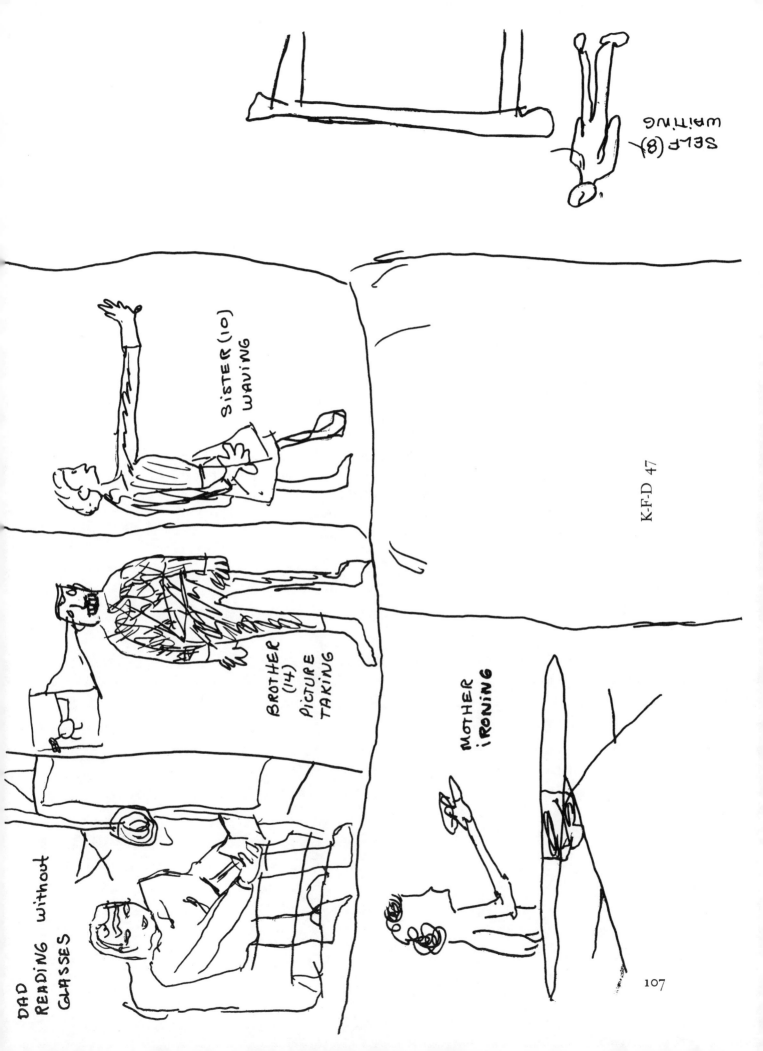

SELF (8)
waiting

SISTER (10) WAVING

BROTHER (14) PICTURE TAKING

DAD READING without GLASSES

MOTHER IRONING

K-F-D 47

107

5. "X"'s—In their struggle for love and warmth, many children are inhibited by a strong conscience or superego. The symbol seen in their drawings is the "X." "X"'s may be placed between, or adjacent to, individual figures and suggest attempts at impulse control. "X"'s may take many forms within the drawings and at times are quite subtle. The "X" may be thought of as force (——>) and counter-force (<——) defining areas of conflict.

The "X" phenomenon may often be displaced. For example, Tom, 13, who did K-F-D 48, was seen because of homosexual activities with his 11-year-old brother. One notes the similarity in the positions of the two heavily shaded boys. One can also see the "X" formed by the feet of the brother, reflecting Tom's conflict and his attempt at control. He also places himself close to the father and mother, who serve as additional controls. Even the 8-year-old sister and 5-year-old brother are armed and threatening. Again, the "X" is very subtle but is placed in the region of conflict. Intense scribbling reflects the boy's anxiety and attempt to control or deny his impulse.

K-F-D 48

5. "X"'s (Cont.)

In K-F-D 49, we see a similar phenomenon. This K-F-D was done by 10-year-old Jack, who was referred because of homosexual activities with his brother. We see again the similarity of the brothers' positions and the turning away. This time, rather than scribbling, there is complete denial of the body. The "X"'s in the drawing are on the source of light or heat—the lamp—and are adjacent to the brother. One notes the surveillance by the parents, particularly the father, who is "watching."

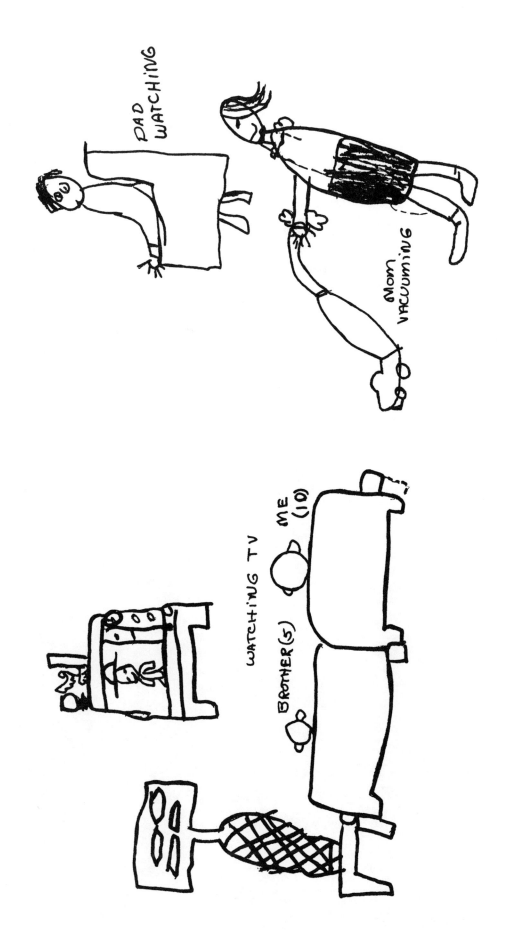

DAD WATCHING

MOM VACUUMING

ME (10)

WATCHING TV

BROTHER(5)

K-F-D 49

111

5. "X"'s (Cont.)

The "X" may be placed in a subtle position, as in K-F-D 50. Twelve-year-old John had feelings about his 14-year-old sister which were quite unacceptable to him. Note the "X" on which she is standing.

5. "X"'s (Cont.)

In a delightful drawing, K-F-D 51, by 9½-year-old Jill, one sees the attempt at control in her strong, but normal, feelings toward her father. While she and her father are connected by a line of force, one notes the "X" below this line, the repetition of the "X" syndrome on the basket and table, and the subtle "X" on the father's chest.

5. "X"'s (Cont.)

At times there is displacement of the "X." For example, in K-F-D 52, by 11-year-old Kathy, we see an "X" above her. In Kathy's case, there was a brother who was very aggressive sexually and toward whom she had great controls. One notes not only the "X" above her, but also the "Keep Out" sign on the door of the clubhouse. The brother is holding a long, phallic-shaped symbol. In this case, the girl was seen because of her fear of being molested by the brother. The parents were divorced, and the mother was out of the home.

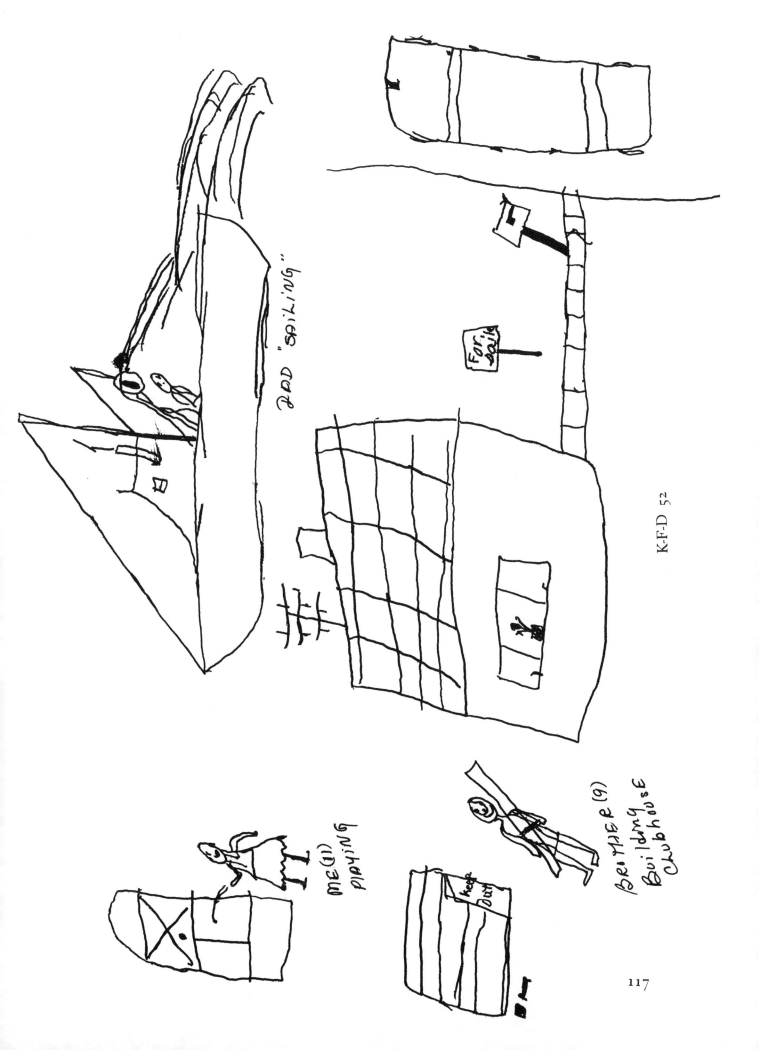

DAD "SAILING"

For Sale

ME(11)
Playing

BROTHER (9)
Building
clubhouse

K-F-D 52

117

5. "X"'s (Cont.)

In K-F-D 53, by adolescent Sally (14½), who was "boy crazy," we see extreme conflict and preoccupation in the area of sexual control. Sally draws herself standing next to her boyfriend with the heat emanating from the phallic-shaped object she holds. We note the "X"'s in the corner of their compartmentalized area. Her brother, who is sexually tempting, is directing a force (the ball) toward an object surrounded by "X"'s. This object is suggestive of female genitalia. There are "X"'s surrounding the object and an "X" on the ball directed toward it. The parents, a source of control, are placed "on the other side" of the paper.

Throughout this chapter we have studied the actions within the K-F-D's. Our next chapter will explore various recurring K-F-D styles.

CHAPTER 5

K-F-D STYLES

INTRODUCTION

In the beginning, most children have a freshness and trustfulness. They express their love naturally and unreservedly without artificial barriers.

NORMAL

Others   Self

Fig. 9—Normal

Things happen and love cannot be expressed naturally, children close themselves off.

COMPARTMENTALIZATION

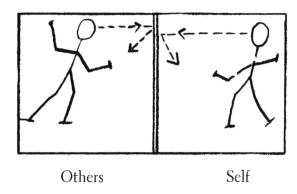

Others   Self

Fig. 10—Compartmentalization

Sometimes we are able to love some people openly, but others bother us, so we encapsulate them.

ENCAPSULATION

Others   Self

Fig. 11—Encapsulation

When our world seems unstable so that we might tumble over, we stabilize it with a firm foundation.

LINING AT THE BOTTOM

Others   Self

Fig. 12—Lining at the Bottom

Sometimes only our relationship to individuals seems unstable, and we underline them.

UNDERLINING INDIVIDUAL FIGURES

Others   Self

Fig. 13—Underlining Individual Figures

Sometimes we become clever and sophisticated and stay on the edge without getting involved.

EDGING

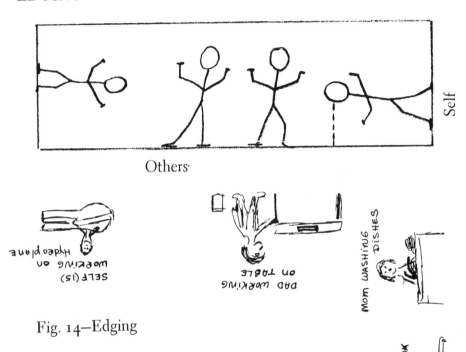

Others·

Self

SELF (15)
working on
Hydeoplane

DAD working
on TABLE

Mom WASHING DISHES

Fig. 14—Edging

SISTER (12)
READING BOOK

BROTHER (4)
LISTENING TO
RECORD

BROTHER (8)
WATCHING TV

Sometimes the world is scary and full of storm clouds, darkness and worry.

LINING AT THE TOP

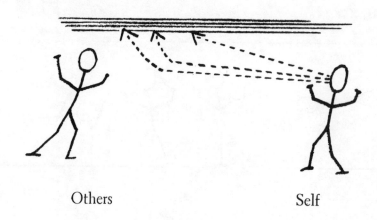

Others   Self

Fig. 15—Lining at the Top

126

FREQUENCY OF STYLES

The frequency of the K-F-D styles found in this book have been combined with those from the introductory Kinetic Family Drawing book (5) to produce Table No. 6.

Rank Order	Style (N=193)	%
1.	Compartmentalization	20.8
2.	Encapsulation	13.0
3.	Lining on the Bottom	12.0
4.	Underlining Individual Figures	9.9
5.	Edging	6.3
6.	Lining on the Top	4.2
7.	Folding Compartmentalization	2.1

Table No. 6—K-F-D Styles

A. DISCUSSION OF K-F-D STYLES

1. *Compartmentalization*—In this style, the child isolates the individual members of the family by putting them in boxes or rectangles or otherwise screening them from each other, as in K-F-D 54. Sometimes this is done in very subtle ways, for example, having one of the siblings jumping rope. This style is typical of social isolates who try to cut off the feeling component between individual members of the family. This is often the beginning stage in withdrawal of the individual or of serious character disorders.

K-F-D 54

Mom
Cooking

Mom

Dad
Water Skiing

Me (10)
Playing
Ball

Me

Sister (7)
Bouncing on Bed

Sister
(7)

129

2. *Encapsulation*—Thirteen-year-old Mike was justifiably terrified of his father and enclosed him in the darkened area of K-F-D 55. The threatening father is isolated from the family by encapsulation. This style is often subtle and the techniques for isolation varied.

DAD MOWING LAWN

WATCHING TV

ME (13)

MOM TYPING

BROTHER (11) PLAYING SOLITAIRE

K-F-D 55

131

2. Encapsulation (Cont.)

Seven-year-old Brian was preoccupied about sleeping with his 13-year-old brother. In K-F-D 56, he encapsulates himself and the brother in bed "sleeping" (?).

133

3. *Lining on the Bottom of the Paper*—This is typical of children who feel instability in the home and are trying to maintain stability by creating a very solid foundation, as in K-F-D 57. The wider the strip at the bottom and the more intense the shading, usually the more severe the disturbance. This is a typical style, for example, of many children in families in the process of divorce or in which there is a great deal of stress and instability.

K-F-D 57

DAD
MOWING
LAWN

MOM
WASHING DISHES

ME (12½)
SWINGING

4. *Underlining Individual Figures*—This style is similar to that of lining on the bottom of the paper. However, the instability reflected by such lining may be focused on an individual figure, in which case only that figure will be heavily underlined. In K-F-D 58, 12-year-old Mike is concerned with the tension between himself and his dominating 15-year-old brother and cutting father. These three figures are underlined emphasizing Mike's instability related to these two dominant older males.

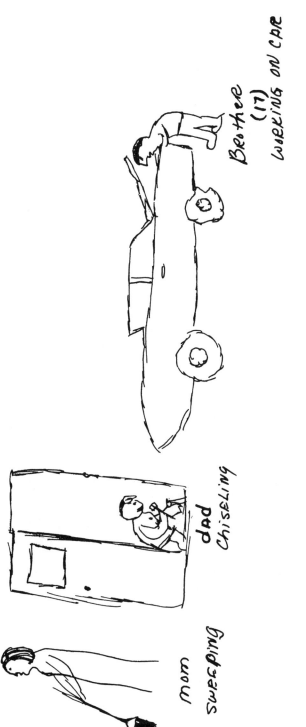

Brother
(17)
working on car

Brother (14)
emptying
garbage

dad
chiseling

mom
building gums

Brother
(15)
mowing lawn

"watch
tinkering"

ME (12)

K-F-D 58

5. *Edging*—Occasionally, a subject will place all the family figures on the periphery of the paper in an edging or rectangular style, as in K-F-D 59. This usually reflects a defensive child who will stay on the periphery of any issue or discussion and one will find resistances against probing at a deeper level. This style is occasionally used to cut off or deny parts of various figures.

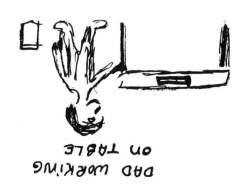

SELF (15)
working on
Hydeoplane

DAD working
on TABLE

Mom WASHING DISHES

SISTER (12)
READING BOOK

KF-D 59

BROTHER (4)
LISTENING TO
RECORD

BROTHER (8)
WATCHING TV

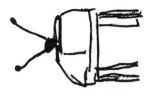

6. *Lining at the Top of the Paper*—Often the top of the paper will be lined by acutely anxious children like Bruce, who produced K-F-D 60.

K-F-D 60

BABY LEFT OUT

ME (6) ON BARS

Mom Sitting Down

DAD

Dog

SISTER (14)

7. *Folding Compartmentalization*—Occasionally, when the children are asked to draw a K-F-D, they will proceed by folding the paper into segments and putting individual figures in these segments, as in K-F-D 61. This is characteristic of children with severe anxieties and fears.

B. EVASIONS

1. *Standing*—Some children will draw everybody, and when asked what the figures are doing, will say they are standing. This is frequently found in children with a mental age below 7 years. It is also characteristic of defensive children. Usually, the children are asked to make another drawing and this time include some form of action or motion as a part of the K-F-D.

2. *Stick Figures*—Occasionally, the child will insist on drawing only stick figures. This is a defense and the child is asked to repeat the drawing, this time making whole figures in action.

In this chapter, we have shown the most obvious and frequent K-F-D styles. Our next chapter will contain a discussion of K-F-D symbols, a much more hazardous area.

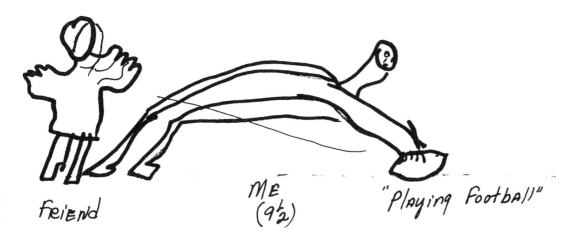

Friend   ME (9½)   "Playing Football"   PAPER FOLDING

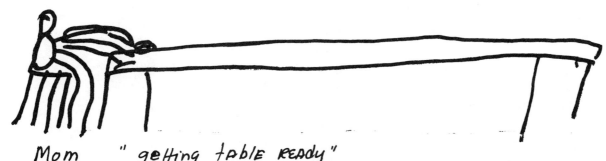

Mom   "getting table ready"
"Resting"

SISTER (8)
"riding
go cart"

K-F-D 61

Dad
"going to work"

143

CHAPTER 6

SYMBOLS

Many times the interpretation of the "meaning of symbols" is subject to overinterpretation and, of course, misinterpretation. Freud (11) emphasized these factors in the seventh chapter of *Interpretation of Dreams* in the discussion of the latent and manifest content of dreams and the distortions and transformations making the interpretations of symbols hazardous. In any attempt at hypothesizing the unconscious expression of any single symbol of a dream or a projective instrument such as a drawing, one must weigh the alternate and sometimes seemingly incompatible interpretations. What is more essential is that the observer be capable, in the frame of reference of his own background, training and skills, to consider the totality of the individual.

Let us consider "Marie" as a case in point. This 7-year-old was brought to the hospital with a history of increasing "nervousness" including mounting night terrors. Her drawing reflected what seemed to be a preoccupation with snakes as a symbol. This, in turn, could be interpreted as a sexual preoccupation consistent with her age, the Oedipal period, or phallic interests. Marie's drawing is K-F-D 62.

It is interesting to point out now that all of Marie's symptoms disappeared following successful treatment for pinworms. If one did not take into consideration the total physical situation, including physical and laboratory diagnosis, as well as her living conditions which exposed her to the possibility of parasitic infestations, the "incorrect," delimited, fragmented psychological interpretation would have been made.

Despite this kind of error, which could appear in oversimplification in the use of symbols, certain symbols do recur in our K-F-D's and are felt, because of their recurrence and consistent

association with the historical physical and clinical material, to be important and worthy of discussion.

We feel it is also important to point out that, in the classified discussion of the meanings of symbols as they appear and reappear in the K-F-D drawings, no attempt is made to completely interpret all of the material as it appears in the drawing. Many drawings hold many different kinds of symbolic meanings. These drawings are picked only to demonstrate the particular kind of symbol discussed in the following classifications.

K-F-D SYMBOLS

"A" 's—In our population the "A" is associated with emphasis on high academic achievement. It is a frequently used symbol and will be pointed out in a number of our K-F-D's.

BEDS—Placement of beds in a K-F-D is relatively rare and is associated with sexual or depressive themes. For example, K-F-D 63, by 13-year-old Ralph, reflects the very significant depression he feels concerning his inability to compete with life in general and particularly with a rather overpowering father figure. Thus, he places himself in bed, with heavy shading reflecting his anxiety.

K-F-D 6₃

BEDS (Cont.)

When everyone in the drawing is in bed, the significance is even greater. In K-F-D 64, 15-year-old Beth depicts her concern with the mother and new stepfather's relationship. In making her K-F-D, she first placed the mother and stepfather in bed and then repeated the theme for the other family members. While this, to some degree, showed her depression, it also reflected her concern about the sexual relationship between her mother and the new male in her family.

mom   stepfather

Bed

Little
stepsis   me

(7)   (15)

BROthER (16)

K-F-D 64

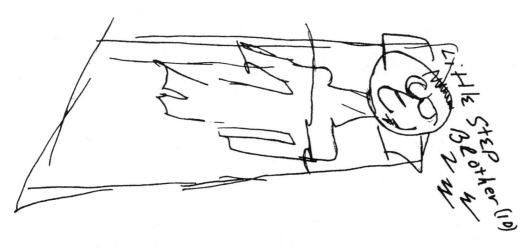

Little Step
Brother (10)

149

BEDS (Cont.)

In K-F-D 65, by 9-year-old Mary, we see a preoccupation with activity surrounding the bed symbol. One notes that the bed has an arm-like quality. All the younger children are "making beds." This mother had never been married, but had children by various fathers. There was much sexual activity in the home which was witnessed by the children. For Mary, the bed was the central and dominant symbol in a disturbed home from which she was later removed.

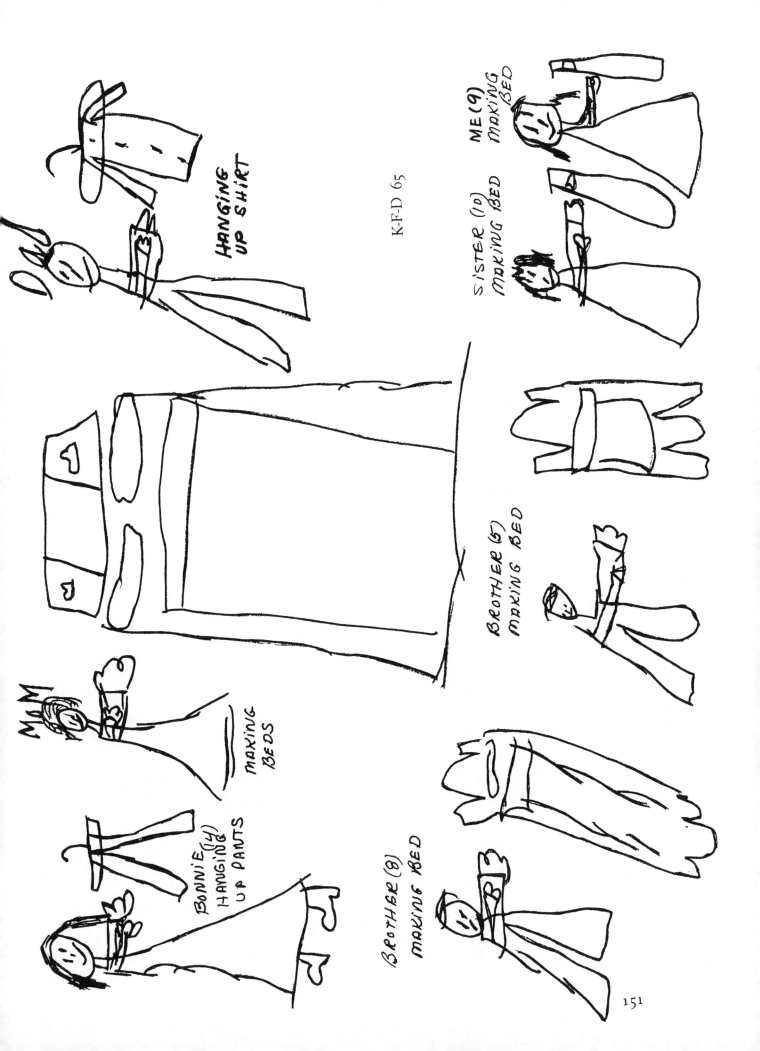

HANGING UP SHIRT

KFD 65

ME (9) MAKING BED

SISTER (10) MAKING BED

BROTHER (5) MAKING BED

MUM MAKING BEDS

BONNIE (14) HANGING UP PANTS

BROTHER (8) MAKING BED

BIKES—Riding bicycles is a common activity of many normal children. When overemphasized, however, the bike may reflect the child's (usually a boy) significant masculine strivings. These strivings become more obvious during adolescence when the power of the bike and motorbike becomes particularly important in reinforcing masculine feelings.

BROOMS—The broom is a recurrent symbol, particularly in the hands of a mother who puts much emphasis on household cleanliness. For example, in K-F-D 66, by 14-year-old Marvin, we see a dominant mother armed with a broom and "above" the other members of the family. The older brothers are engaged in repetition of the mother's cleaning. One pleases this mother by being "clean" in thought and deed.

The mother with the broom is often associated with the "witchy" mother.

COUCH

mom

K-F-D 66

RADIO

DUST PAN

BROTHER (20)

FATHER

MOP

BROTHER (16½)

ME
(14)

BUTTERFLIES—In our population, this symbol is associated with the search for illusive love and beauty.

CATS—In many K-F-D's, particularly those of girls, cats are a dominant symbol. Preoccupation with cats is often symbolic of conflict in identification with the mother. The furry "cuddliness" of the cat, combined with its teeth and claws, creates a symbol related to ambivalence and conflict.

Abigail, 10, was said to be quite a tomboy, and the family was concerned about this. She was very close to the father. Abby's drawing is K-F-D 67. Note the shading which reflects her identification with her father and her anxiety about this identification. The "X" phenomenon, or attempt to control impulse, is drawn on the father. Note, however, the similarity between the "X" and the cat's whiskers. The drawing suggests some generalization from the father to the cat. It was noted that Abby loved cats. She kept them in her bedroom and slept with them, thus apparently sublimating some of her interest toward the father by means of the cat.

my family

MY sister

Me (ia)

"Mommy"

"Poppy"

tom my - our
cat

CATS (Cont.)

A simple form of interest in the cat is shown in K-F-D 68. In this family, the stepfather and mother were very close, and 5-year-old Jerry was extremely jealous of this relationship. He kept his cat in his room at night and apparently transferred some of his affection from the "planting" parents to the cat.

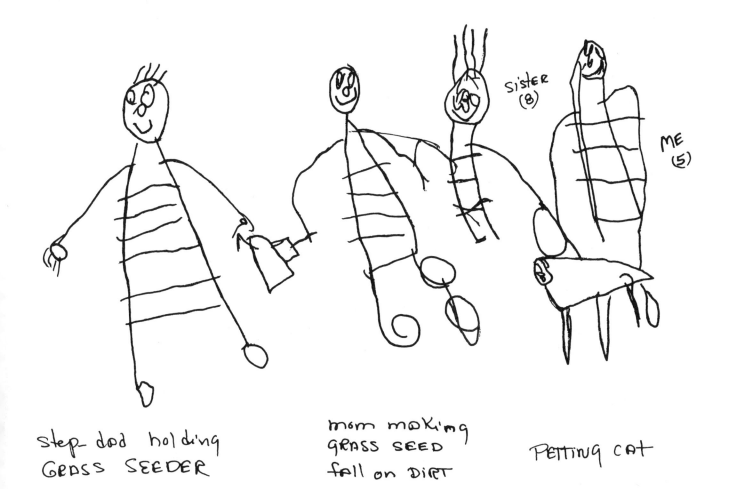

step dad holding
GRASS SEEDER

mom making
GRASS SEED
fall on DIRT

PETTING CAT

sister
(8)

ME
(5)

K-F-D 68

CATS (Cont.)

In K-F-D 69, we see a little girl, 11, who came to us because of the parents' complaint that she was extremely anxious. Jane was very competitive with the mother for the father's affection. The father was engaged in rather dangerous work, and the little girl was very concerned about him. She seemed to transfer some of this love and concern in her conflict with the mother to her preoccupation with cats.

DAD NOT WORKING

SISTER(8) SETTING TABLE

MA COOKING

SELF(11) PLAYING WITH CAT

K-F-D 69

CATS (Cont.)

Occasionally, when love and identification are not possible, the child becomes preoccupied with cats and actually identifies closely with the role of the cat in the family.

In K-F-D 70, we see an 8-year-old girl whose father has been quite ill and depressed. Both parental figures were quite distant and difficult for Sharon to love, so she tended to identify with the cat.

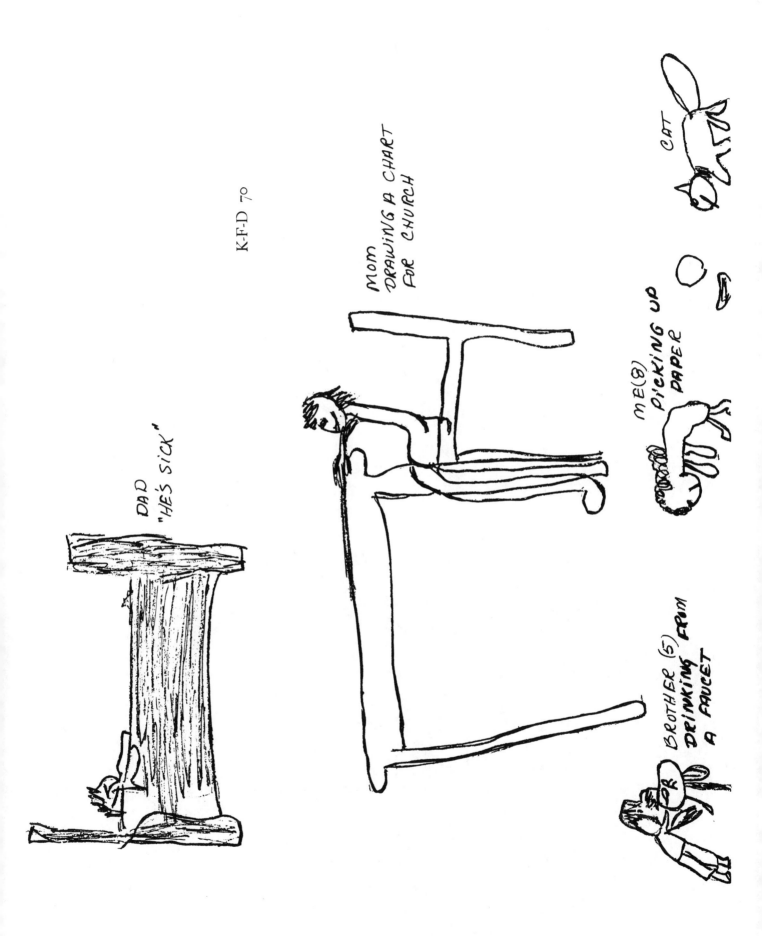

K-F-D 70

DAD
"HE'S SICK"

MOM
DRAWING A CHART
FOR CHURCH

ME(8) PICKING UP
PAPER

CAT

BROTHER (5)
DRINKING FROM
A FAUCET

CATS (Cont.)

In K-F-D 71, by 11-year-old Karen, we see great importance attached to cats. It is noted that when Karen started the K-F-D, she first folded the paper into four parts. This little girl was extremely anxious. Her parents were in the midst of a divorce. Her father was mentally ill and her mother, who was also quite disturbed, had an alcohol problem. Karen was very depressed at the time she was seen. She was leaving for Italy with her mother —a second separation from her father. Karen did not receive adequate love from either parent. She was quite angry with her mother. Note the size of the cat in comparison to the Self and to the mother. The cat, in this stage of her development, was much more important to Karen, and much more satisfying in terms of warmth and love, than the mother.

K-F-D 71

163

CATS (Cont.)

In K-F-D 72, by 8½-year-old Bruce, we see a different theme. His father was an extremely punishing man with whom Bruce could not compete. He tended, however, to identify with Dad's strength. Thus, the father and boy are doing the same thing and competing through the kicking activities. Note, however, that the father's box soars high in the air, while the boy's is close to the ground. Bruce was quite preoccupied with cats when we saw him. Note the mother is cuddling the cat, which is perhaps what the boy wanted for himself. He seemed to identify with the cat and was very angry with both parents.

K-F-D 72

DAD
KICKING BOX

MOM
HOLDING CAT

SISTER (16)
WALKING

(8½) ME
KICKING
BOX

165

CATS (Cont.)

In adolescents we get extremely complicated dynamics in terms of the meaning of cats. Often the dynamics are related to girls having difficulty in identification with their mothers, with conflict and ambivalence in this area. K-F-D 73 was done by 16½-year-old Judy, who had withdrawn and become extremely shy and depressed. She tended to identify with her 6-year-old sister. Her mother had been ill, and Judy drew herself watching her mother. In real life, however, she had regressed to the level of the sister, who is "running backward trying to get the cat to come to her." Judy was a girl who did not dare show anger toward her mother. She displaced it not only to her sister, but also to the activities of the sister in the drawing.

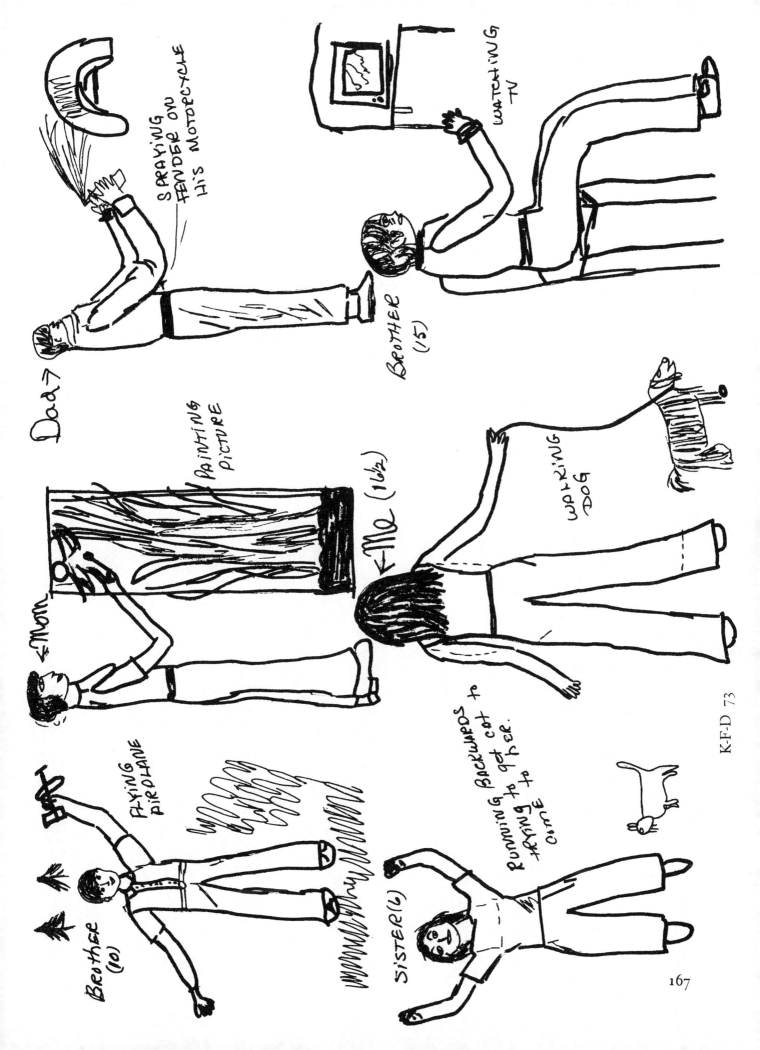

Dad > SPRAYING FENDER ON HIS MOTORCYCLE

BROTHER (15) WATCHING TV

Mom > PAINTING PICTURE

< Me (16½) WALKING DOG

BROTHER (10) FLYING AIRPLANE

SISTER (6) RUNNING BACKWARDS TRYING TO GET CAT TO COME TO HER.

KF-D 73

167

CATS (Cont.)

In K-F-D 74, we see 12-year-old Martha, who loves cats. She is a competitive girl, placing herself "above" the busy, P.T.A. mother, toward whom she is very ambivalent. Note the shading below the planting father's waist and continuation of the shading on the cats moving toward the mouse hole. Martha is busily sublimating her striving for Dad's love by "making a flower mural" and perhaps by her great fascination with cats.

CATS (Cont.)

In K-F-D 75, we see the K-F-D of 17-year-old Kris, who was described as the "most popular girl in her high school class." She was brought to our attention because of nightmares about cats attacking her. Kris tended to see herself as ugly, which she was not, and quite unable to compete with her mother, who in reality was quite homely and very obese. The girl could not accept competition with her mother, yet she had a great deal of feeling for her. She was very close to her father. The cat became the central theme in her psychopathology. The anger she felt toward her mother was completely unacceptable, and she tended to deny and repress it. It is noted that the cat is attached to the mother and is a part of the mother complex. Kris' destructive, hostile feelings toward Mother and her anxiety about her own sexuality results in the de-sexualization of Kris and the overcompensating beauty of the mother.

Brother

Mom

Dad

SAM

Sister
(14)

"Arranging
flowers"

K-F-D 75

CLOWNS—A preoccupation with clowns is often seen in children who have significant feelings of inferiority.

K-F-D 76 was done by 9-year-old Eric, who displayed significant feelings of inadequacy. He had an overpowering father of whom he was very fearful. Eric tended to regress and act much younger. In his drawing he is in the position of a young child watching the TV, which is showing the clown with whom he identifies. This boy had a history of school failure. He also found it very difficult to please the father. He showed many other indications that he felt inadequate.

CLOWN

SISTER (10)

ME (9) WATCHING TV

DAD WATCHING TV

BROTHER (7)

K-F-D 76

CRIBS—A baby in the family is an event which usually causes jealousy in the other siblings. K-F-D 77 reflects many of the dynamics in the reactions of a child to a new, favored baby. This drawing was done by 7½-year-old Billy, and we note how the baby is the center of the family's attention. Billy is upside down; apparently this is the way his world is at this time, with a 3-month old baby in the family. We note the crib in which the baby is placed has repetitive lines and some elements of the cross-hatching seen in more obsessive-compulsive cases. In addition, Billy is throwing something in the garbage can. This is a recurrent K-F-D method of evicting the intruder on the family's peace and quiet. Little children get rid of things in the house that are "nasty" or "dirty" by throwing them in the garbage can and, of course, many children have told their parents they would like to put the new baby in the garbage can. This is a repeated symbol in the new baby syndrome and will be discussed further under "Garbage Cans."

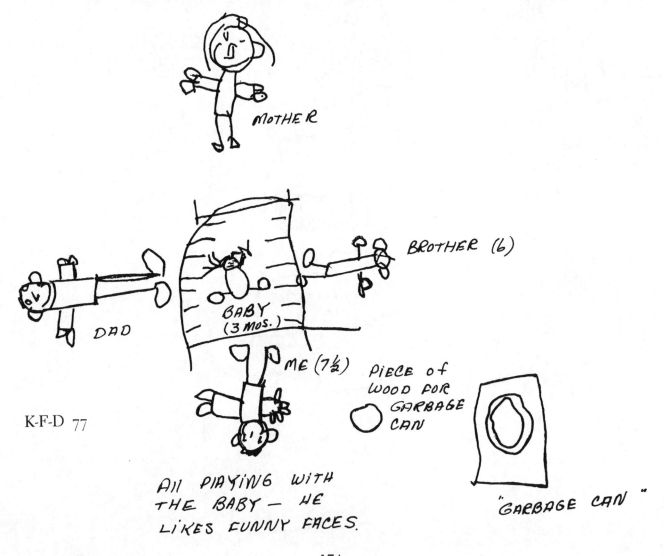

MOTHER

BROTHER (6)

DAD

BABY (3 MOS.)

ME (7½)

PIECE of WOOD FOR GARBAGE CAN

K-F-D 77

"GARBAGE CAN"

All PLAYING WITH THE BABY — HE LIKES FUNNY FACES.

174

CRIBS (Cont.)

Sometimes a new baby can interfere with schoolwork. K-F-D 78, by 11-year-old Ruth, reflects such a situation. Ruth kept calling home to see if the new baby was all right, and she found numerous excuses to come home from school. Note that the parents' faces are turned away from the baby, and although the girl is studying, she is faced in the general direction of the baby. It is noted that the crib is the largest symbol or figure in the drawing and dominates the girl's thinking. The heavy marking on the crib reflects a tendency toward denial or anxieties in relation to the baby.

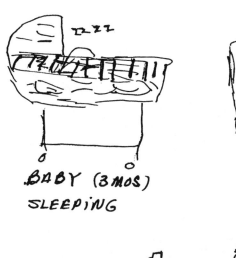

.BABY (3 MOS)
SLEEPING

DAD
READING PAPER

MOM
COOKING

ME (11)
STUDYING

K-F-D 78

CRIBS (Cont.)

In K-F-D 79, done by 8-year-old Allen, we note the relative size of the crib (playpen), which is placed very close to the mother. While the mother is engaged in cooking, one notes the "on-off" above the stove, as if the mother can turn her nurturance or affection on and off. The boy is running frantically in the direction of the cooking—or mother—but the large crib in between would seem to be a barrier. It is noted that the threatening father is on the reverse side of the picture "mowing the lawn."

K-F-D 79

CRIBS (Cont.)

In K-F-D 80, 9-year-old Bill reflects his preoccupation with the health and well-being of the 2-month-old baby. He has symptoms of fear that something may happen to the baby, and he wants to stay home from school. We see that, in addition to his sitting and facing the baby, the crib is repeated in the legs of the TV set and is also in the TV picture, reflecting Bill's preoccupation and obsession concerning the well-being of the baby. The crib symbol, then, is repeated three times and the boy is carefully watching all three in the drawing.

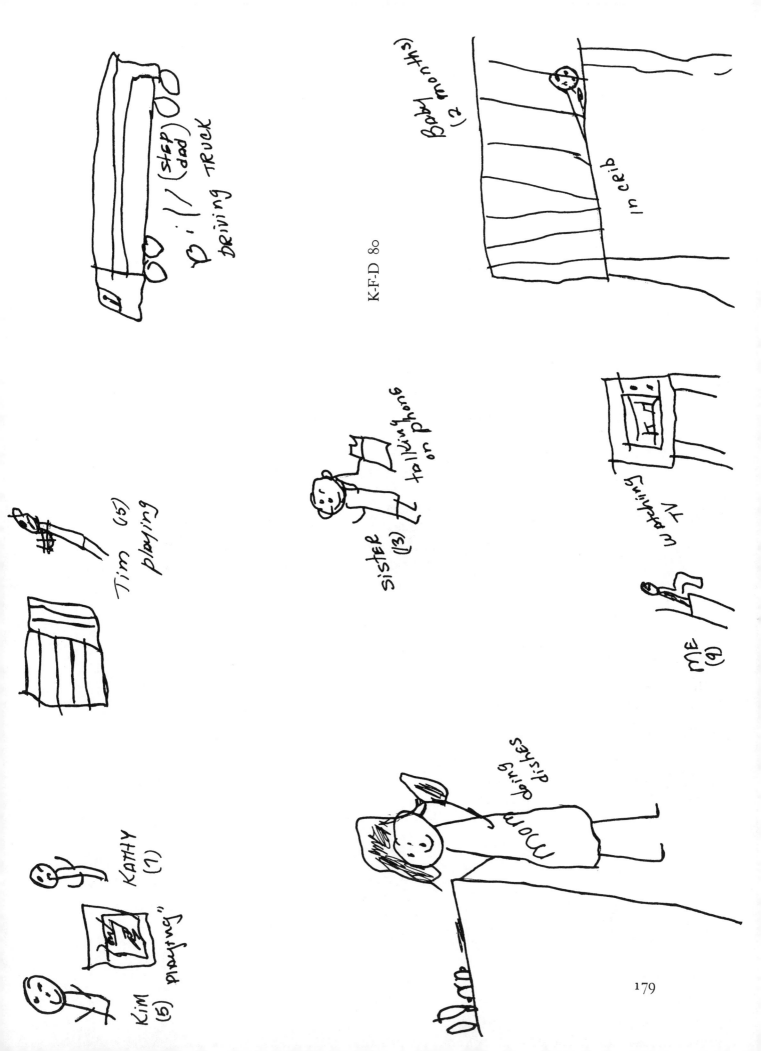

K-F-D 80

179

DIRT—The theme of digging or shoveling dirt will be repeated throughout the K-F-D's. Dirt, of course, has a negative connotation and children are often admonished for having dirty thoughts or dirty clothes, and the figures in our K-F-D's associated with dirt usually have similar negative feelings attached.

DRUMS—Drums are a symbol of displaced anger. K-F-D 81, done by angry 7-year-old Joshua, reflects this theme. This boy is quite disturbed and very displeased about the attention paid a 14-month-old child in the family. We note the sister playing vigorously on the drums. She is standing on a box and is a very domineering sort of person. Joshua is also pounding on the roof, but much less effectively. We note the baby is seen as banging a balloon, although it would appear that the baby is receiving a blow. There is disturbance in relation to the mother, who is drawn in the farthest compartment from Joshua. The underpinning below the mother suggests the boy's feelings of instability in relation to her at this time. The total theme of the pounding, including the drumming, is very frequently seen in children with much anger who have difficulty expressing it openly and who tend to displace this anger to the drum.

DRUMS (Cont.)

In K-F-D 82, we see 8-year-old Jill, who has had a great deal of difficulty in reading and who feels extremely inadequate. We note the circular placement of the family members. The drums are being played by the brother. Jill could not express her angry feelings associated with her school failure. The "edge style" reveals her tendency to avoid situations. She displaces her feelings through activities such as drumming, in which she is very interested.

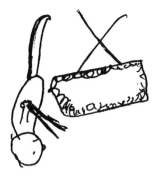

BROTHER (11) PLAYING DRUMS

BROTHER (14) ← SKIS

SISTER (10) WALKING

K-F-D 82

sitting and singing

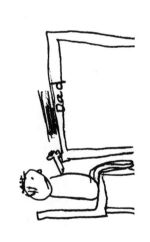

Dad

ME (8) READING

DRUMS (Cont.)

K-F-D 83 was done by a very angry 10-year-old boy. Jim is very distant from his father, who has been ill. He has a younger brother who is ascendent and is elevated by the stool. Brother is very successful in competing for the father's affection. Jim is very angry with the brother; he also feels extremely inadequate. Note the difference in the size of the two figures. Jim tends to sublimate his anger and his need for ascendency through his drums.

Big Sister (13) "Playing Guitar"

Cooking Dinner

Mom

Me (10) "Playing Drums"

K-F-D 83

FATHER

sick

BROTHER (4) playing BASKETBALL

185

ELECTRICITY—This symbol is usually associated with extreme need for warmth and love. It has an element of control and, if the preoccupation is extreme, may be associated with poor reality testing, as in schizoid conditions.

FIRE—There are at least two meanings associated with fire as a symbol in our K-F-D's: (1) the need for warmth and love, with the usual interpretation of other light themes, although the intensity is much greater; (2) the fact that love may turn into hate is also reflected in the fire, often seen as a destructive force. As is well known, most fire setters are passive-aggressive types of personalities, most frequently boys with a great deal of repressed anger which is often intertwined with sexual gratification through firesetting. The need for love, if unmet, leads to great intensity and destructive tendencies, as seen in the fire themes and symbols.

FLOWERS—Flowers represent love of beauty and the growth process. In little girls, the flower below the waist often suggests feminine identification, as in K-F-D 84, by 12-year-old Margie.

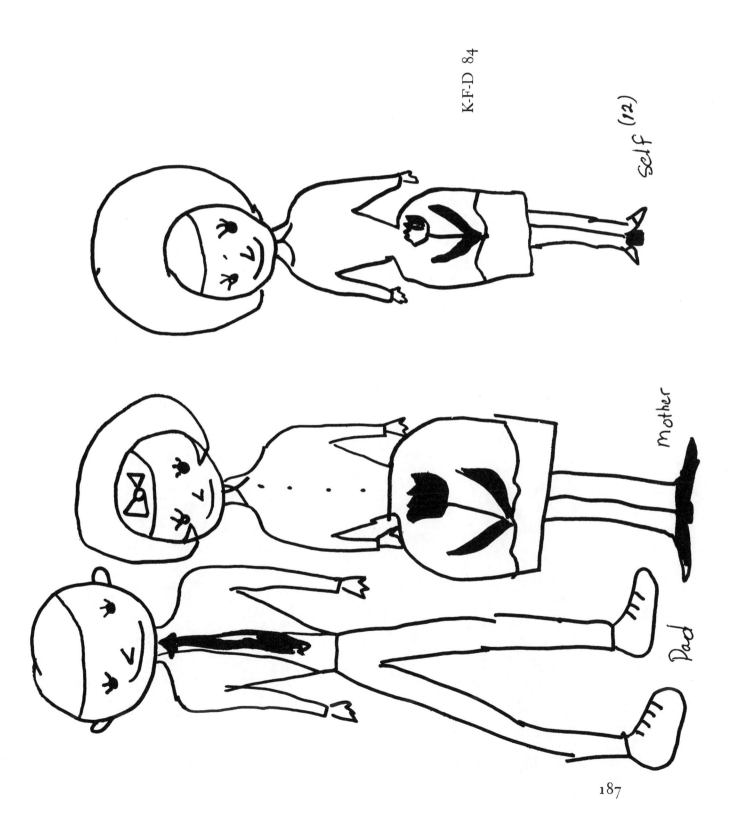

KFD-84

Self (12)

Mother

Dad

FLOWERS (Cont.)

At times the search for love and beauty, as symbolized by the flower, may be a very distant goal. K-F-D 85, produced by Jimmy, a deprived boy of 9½, shows great interest in the nurturance of the cooking mother, but we also see the central symbol of the flower telling us of his need for love. Boys who use this symbol, of course, are more prone to feminine identification and goals. Jimmy was much closer to the mother and was somewhat feminine. It is noted that the father is grouped with the other two brothers and there is a barrier between Jimmy and them symbolized by the flower.

K-F-D 85

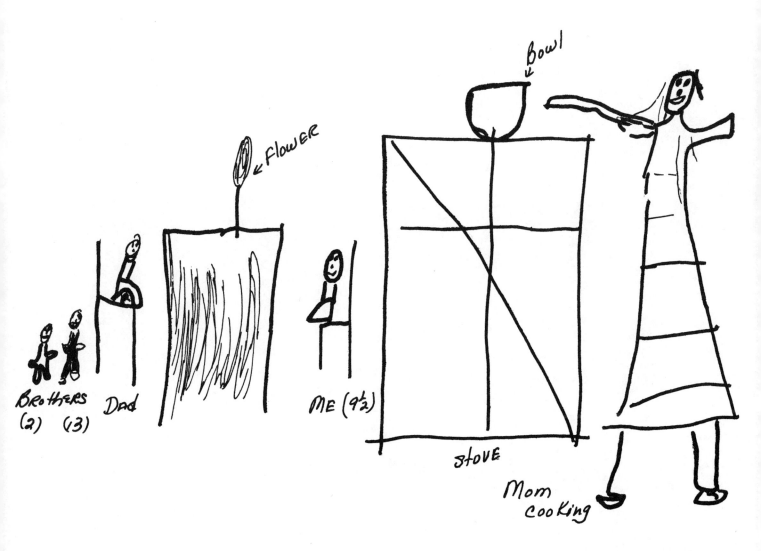

Bowl

Flower

Brothers
(2) (3)   Dad

ME (9½)

STOVE

Mom
cooking

GARBAGE—For many young children, taking out the garbage is equivalent to taking out the unwanted and "dirty" parts of the family existence. It is most frequently found in the K-F-D's when there are new babies in the family. The arrival of a new baby is often completely disrupting for a child, and he displays significant regressive tendencies.

In K-F-D 86, we see some of the turmoil reflected in the drawing of 7½-year-old Charles, burdened by a new arrival in his family. Note how close the new baby is to the father! Charles is frantically trying to get closer to the parents. Note the very distorted arm of the mother reaching directly over to the garbage can. This boy actually asked the parents to put the baby in the garbage after they came home from the hospital.

Bobby (9)
standing on
Bottle.

Cathy Rickling
(sous 3)

DAD trying to
Trying to
SEE what is
mom Doing

KF-D 86

me (7½)
Trying to
keep from
falling HE HAS
Tree climbed

mom
stretching
HER ARMS to put
garbage
in can.

GARBAGE (Cont.)

K-F-D 87, by 7½-year-old Sharon, reflects extreme stress at having a new child in the family which she cannot accept. When asked to produce the K-F-D, she folded the paper into four sections, showing her great disturbance in the interrelationships between members of the family. She could not draw the baby and insisted on putting it on the other side of the paper. She is busily engaged in carrying garbage to the underlined garbage can, which is taller than she is and a major symbol in the K-F-D. One suspects that she is symbolically removing from the house that which is undesirable to her, and at this particular stage of her development, that something is the baby.

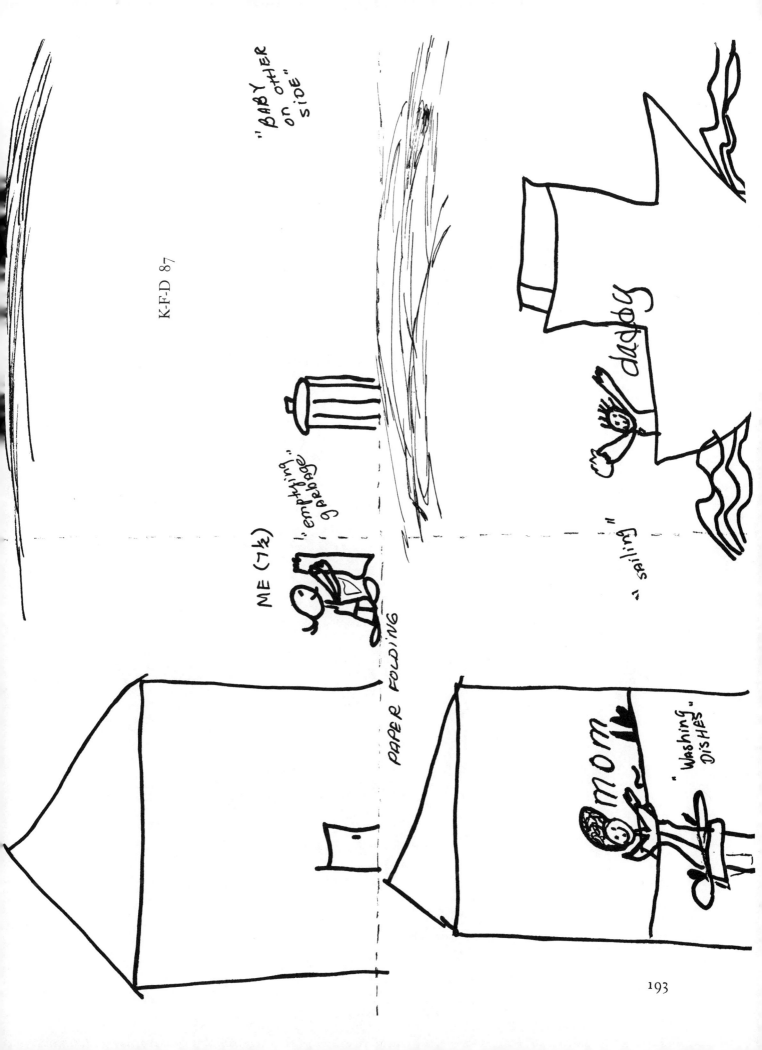

193

GARBAGE (Cont.)

In K-F-D 88, we see 9-year-old Frank, who has a new baby in his family. Frank showed regressive behavior during this period. He resented sharing the little warmth in this large family with the baby. In his K-F-D, he is engaged in taking the garbage out. It is emphasized, again, that the garbage theme is most frequent when there are young babies in the family, or when a new competitor, such as a foster child, enters the family.

MOM
VACUUMING

BROTHER (4)
PLAYING ARMY

SISTER (11)
CLEANING TABLE

MY SELF (9)
TAKING OUT
THE GARBAGE

DAD
DRINKING
COFFEE

BROTHER (7)
EMPTYING DISHWASHER

BROTHER (2)
GETTING SOMETHING FROM
REFRIGERATOR

BABY
(5 MOS.)

BROTHER (10)
SWEEPING
FLOOR

K-F-D 88

195

GARBAGE (Cont.)

K-F-D 89 was produced by extremely competitive 6-year-old Scott. The 1-year-old brother was an extreme threat to him, and while he is still busily competing with the two older sisters, the garbage can next to the mother suggests that he would like to get rid of the 1-year-old, who is a threat to him in terms of the parents' attention.

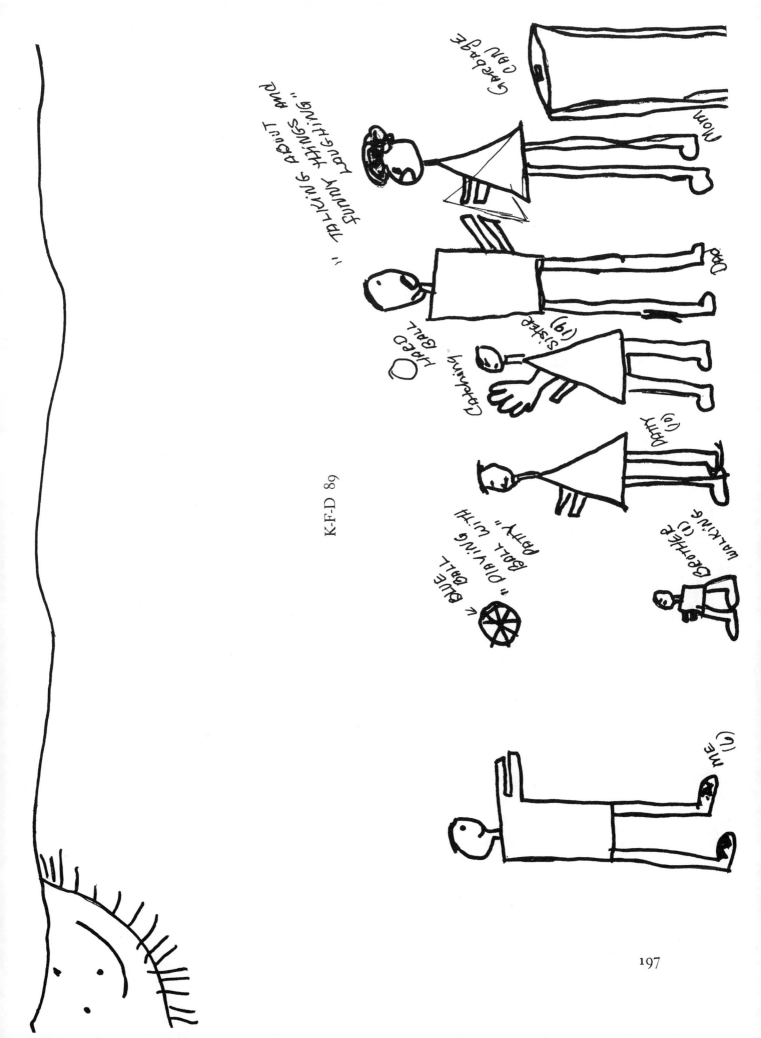

K-F-D 89

197

GARBAGE (Cont.)

Occasionally, the garbage theme is seen in children without infants in the family. It is most frequently associated with significant guilt about feelings of rivalry and ambivalence toward a younger sibling. Eight-year-old Tony, who drew K-F-D 90, was extremely jealous of his 6-year-old sister. Tony was continually after her, taunting her verbally and "pestering" her. One notes the compartmentalization in this family and Tony taking the garbage out. The placement of his eye suggests that he is looking back at his sister. From the dynamics in the family, one suspects that the garbage theme, while it has continued longer than usual with this child, is related to the dynamics between Tony and his younger sister.

SISTER (6)
PUTTING DISHES AWAY

SELF (8)
TAKING OUT GARBAGE

BROTHER (14)
DRYING DISHES

MOM
DRIVING
CAR

DAD
GETTING
DOWN NAILS
TO FIX
DOOR

K-F-D 90

199

HEAT—Heat symbolizes the need for love and warmth.

IRONING BOARD—The ironing board may be used as a symbol in a number of ways. The most striking and perhaps most common is the ironing board with the "X" used to cross out the mother. This is often done by adolescent boys with a good deal of conflict and ambivalence toward the maternal figure.

When the ironing board is drawn by girls, it is usually not drawn with an "X" through the body, as in the boys' drawings. The "X" is displaced outside the Self and associated with ambivalence toward other members of the family.

Previous examples have been given of the ironing board used in "X"ing out the maternal figure.

It is often used by girls, for example, as seen in K-F-D 91. This picture was drawn by Sarah, 8, who had great ambivalence and anger toward her younger brother. She is very annoyed with him and can openly discuss this. The iron in this case seems to be related to the intensity of her feeling toward him and feelings of rejection on the part of the mother. It is noted that the mother is vacuuming and seems more concerned with orderliness in the house and the external environment than with Sarah.

My Family

Father yelling
"Let me
come it?
do it"

Vacuuming

MA

K-F-D 91

ME (8)
"IRONING"

Brother (7)
"Pulling"
my hair

201

IRONING BOARD (Cont.)

In K-F-D 92, we see a family in which there is much anger. The girl producing the drawing shows her sister ironing, while she is vacuuming. There is a lot of shading below the mother's waist. Notice the downturned mouths in the family. This is, indeed, an unhappy family. The intensity of the feelings is reflected by the symbol of the iron with its intense heat, suggesting an equally intense need for love.

KF-D 92

sister (12)
ironing

ME (10)
VACUUMING

BROTHER (14)
MAD AND
WASHING
DISHES

Mom making bed

JUMP ROPE—K-F-D 93 was produced by 14-year-old Peter, who tried very hard to capture the mother's attention from a vivacious 7-year-old sister. The sister is a great rival for the boy, and he spends a lot of time and energy keeping her away from the mother. Note the encapsulation of the sister and the boy facing her and placing himself between the mother and the rope-jumping sister.

Mom cooking

Me (14) skiing

K-F-D 93

Sister (7) "jumping rope"

Dad "doing paper work"

Brother (11) "playing basketball"

JUMP ROPE (Cont.)

In K-F-D 94, produced by 10-year-old Heather, we see compartmentalization. Heather is a "loner" who relates to the family animals. She has always been very jealous of the next younger sister, who is now 8 years old and is pictured close to the mother. The encapsulation of this figure, which makes one focus on it visually, suggests she is the actual center of Heather's attentions and conflicts. Note the sister is pictured as quite beautiful, while the Self is homely, although the opposite is true.

SELF(10)

my Dog

walking with dog

K-F-D 94

Mom

cleaning up Kitchen cabinet

F
O

Sister(8)

sister 3

BROTHER(9)

JUMP ROPE (Cont.)

In K-F-D 95, we see 13-year-old Annie, who desires to be grownup and independent. She is extremely rivalrous with her 21-year-old sister, wanting to tag along and imitate her. On the other hand, there is a lot of tension in her relationship to the younger sisters. She encapsulates all of them—one with a jump rope and the other two with swings.

K-F-D 95

MOM

DAD SUNBATHING

BROTHER (9) RIDING BIKE

ME (13)

PLAYING BALL

SISTER (21)

SISTER (11)

SISTER (10)

SWINGING

SISTER (8) JUMPING ROPE

JUMP ROPE (Cont.)

K-F-D 96 shows 12-year-old Jane, who encapsulates herself. It is noted that she has an extremely threatening father and older brother. In this case, the jump rope is used as a protective device for the Self.

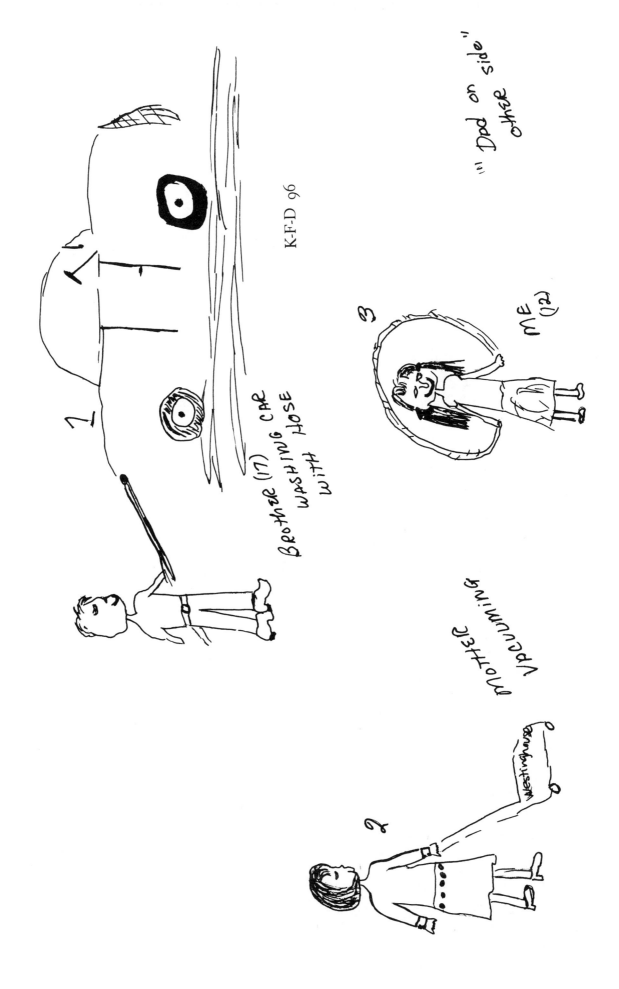

KF-D 96

"Dad on other side"

ME (12)

Brother (17) WASHING CAR WITH HOSE

MOTHER VACUUMING

westinghouse

KITES—Kites, and sometimes balloons, are symbols used by children who are attempting to get out of or above a family environment seen as restrictive. This symbol is associated with the desire for escape and freedom.

In K-F-D 97, we see Louise, who has school problems. We note the older sister, who is surrounded by "A" 's. She is favored by the family because of her success in school. The father, mother and grandmother are watching her and, in actual life, supervise very closely. Louise places the dog between herself and the family as a barrier and attaches herself to a kite. If this theme continues into adolescence, Louise will probably "take off."

213

KITES (Cont.)

In K-F-D 98, by 10-year-old Gerald, we see a different theme. The boy has a very restrictive, punishing father. Despite this, Gerald loves him and seems to identify with him. Although he is following in the father's footsteps, at times he would like to be free of this ominous, restrictive figure, and the kite is symbolic of his desire to be free and ascendent.

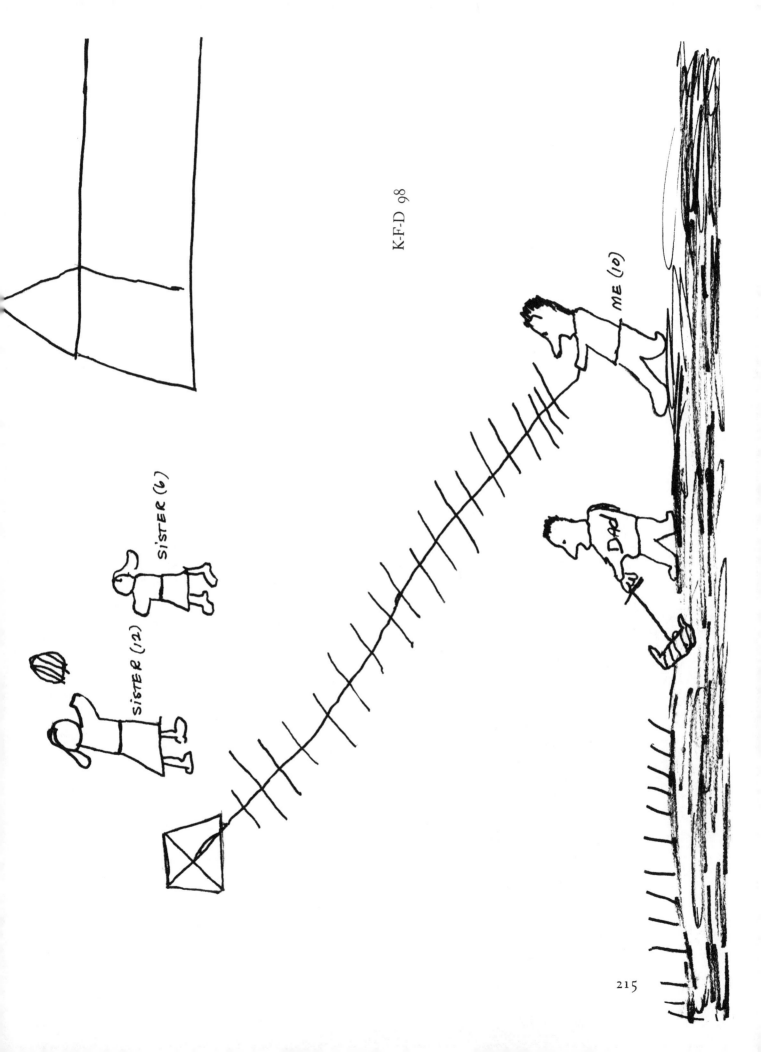

SISTER (6)

SISTER (12)

ME (10)

DAD

K-F-D 98

215

LADDERS—Ladders are associated with tension and precarious balance. In K-F-D 99, George, a rebellious young man with a distant, punishing father, places the father on a ladder, reflecting the tension in the father-son relationship. The "Me" is rotated and his eyes are fixated on a TV space program.

K-F-D 99

DAD PAINTING

BROTHER (13) Coming in House

SPACE MAN

ME (14) WATCHING TV

BROTHER (18) KICKING

MOM FIXING CURTAIN

SISTER (7) EMPTYING WASTE PAPER

BROTHER KICKING (23)

LADDERS (Cont.)

In K-F-D 100, we see extremely competitive 10½-year-old Roger. Note the "A"'s associated with the two younger siblings and their encapsulation. The boy has attempted to assume a dominant role in the home and is very competitive with the father. This competition frightens him, and his relation to the father is a tense one, as reflected in the ascendent father's precarious stance on the ladder.

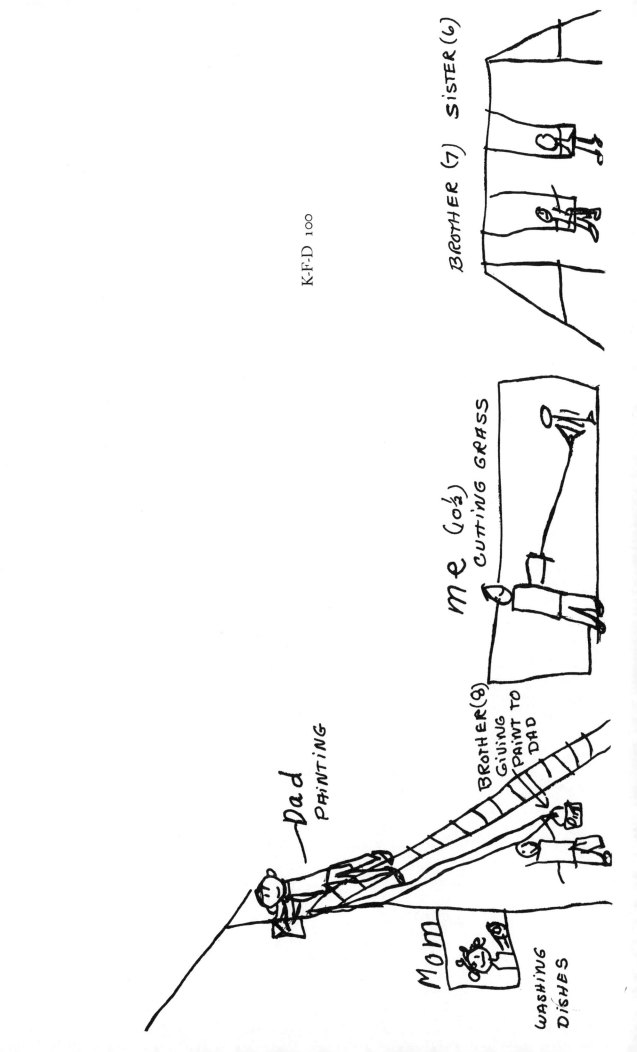

BROTHER (7) SISTER (6)

K-F-D 100

me (10½)
CUTTING GRASS

Dad
PAINTING

BROTHER (8)
GIVING
PAINT TO
DAD

Mom

WASHING
DISHES

LADDERS (Cont.)

K-F-D 101, by 10-year-old Tina, shows her in an identical pose with her extremely over-controlling "Mom." Tina has a symbiotic relation to Mom, seen in their identical position and action. She also reflects the extreme tension between the parents with "Dad" balanced precariously on the ladder.

DAD STANDING ON LADDER

K-F-D 101

PAPER FOLDING

ME (10)

Walking Dog

DOG walking

MOM walking dog

LADDERS (Cont.)

In K-F-D 102, we see 8-year-old Tom, who has feelings of. inadequacy and who is very threatened by his oldest brother. Tom was unable to draw himself; however, he is in the attic "above" the climbing older brother. The tension between them is reflected in the balancing of the brother on the ladder. While he is above the brother, this position of superiority produces tension.

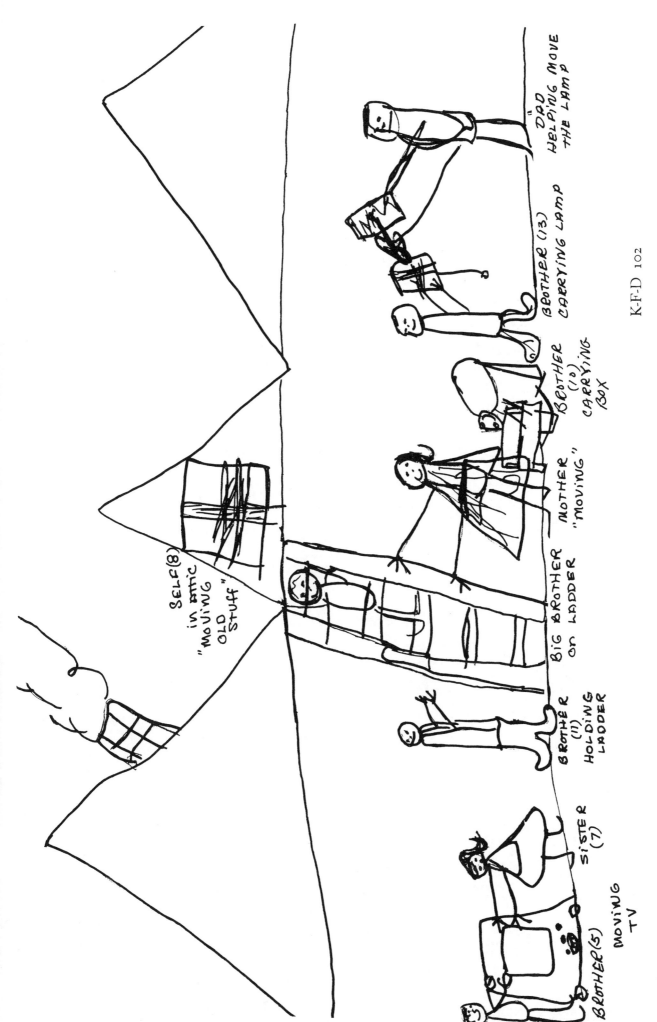

SELF(8) in attic "MOVING OLD STUFF"

"DAD" HELPING MOVE THE LAMP

BROTHER (13) CARRYING LAMP

BROTHER (10) CARRYING BOX

MOTHER "MOVING"

BIG BROTHER ON LADDER

BROTHER (11) HOLDING LADDER

SISTER (7)

BROTHER(5) MOVING TV

K-F-D 102

223

LAMPS—Lamps are a symbol of warmth and love.

LAWNMOWERS—The lawnmower is a cutting symbol, most frequently associated with castrating figures. In many of our K-F-D's, the father will be drawn with this symbol. It is usually depicted by a boy. There are many variations, however.

K-F-D 103 was done by 20-year-old Dianne, who has always felt threatened by her oldest brother, who is very vindictive. He is the largest and most threatening figure in the drawing. He is directly above her, and the lawnmower suggests the cutting quality of his relationship to her.

LAWNMOWERS (Cont.)

In a family in which the father is quite distant, the oldest boy may assume his role and become the castrator. In K-F-D 104, we see 11-year-old Billy, the oldest son, directing his energies (mowing) toward controlling the 14-year-old sister with whom he is competitive for dominance within the sibling relationship.

K-F-D 104

"that was going
to be me"

BrotHER(9)
Playing Ball

me(11)
Mowing Lawn

"shopping"

Mom

shoE

sister(14)

"WASHING
DiSHES"

Dad

"DRIVING"

227

LAWNMOWERS (Cont.)

In K-F-D 105, we see Tim, 9½, who places himself close to
the parents. He is unable to compete with a very domineering
12-year-old sister, who is seen as "cutting."

DAD
CARRYING
GROCERIES

MOM
CARRYING
GROCERIES

ME (9½)
CARRYING BUCKET
OF PAINT

SISTER (14)
CUTTING LAWN

SISTER (13)
WASHING
WINDOWS

BROTHER (7)
WASHING CAR

LAWNMOWERS (Cont.)

In K-F-D 106, by 17-year-old Phillip, we see more of a wish fulfillment. Phillip had an extremely threatening and punishing father. At times this boy wanted to assume a dominant role but was very threatened by such a role. He tends to compartmentalize the family, placing his mother above him. He is directing his energies toward the younger brother and controlling him in the same way the father has controlled and threatened him. The underlining at the base of the drawing reflects the extreme tension in this family.

KF-D 106

231

LEAVES—Leaves are associated with dependency. They are a symbol of that which clings to the source of nurturance.

K-F-D 107, done by 13-year-old Lennie, reflects the subtle aspect of the leaf symbol in many drawings. This boy was an isolate who felt left out of the family. The tree in the drawing serves as a barrier between him and the rest of the family. The 14-year-old brother is among the leaves of the tree. The 9-year-old brother is much closer to the father. He looks like the father, and in Lennie's view is closer to the father. We note that this brother is raking leaves. Lennie has much resentment toward the brother because he feels the brother has received more warmth and love from the parents, particularly the father.

BROTHER (14) TREE
CLIMBING

ME (13) PLAYING
BASEBALL
to
base
ball

MOM HANGING
UP CLOTHES
TOWELS

DAD WORKING ON
HIS TRUCK

Garden

BROTHER (9)
RAKING UP
LEAVES

SISTER (6)
RIDING
HER BIKE

K-F-D 107

LEAVES (Cont.)

K-F-D 108 was made by 10½-year-old Judy, whose parents had just been divorced. The father had custody of her at the time. We note the distant mother coming from the store, with the road used to separate her from the family. The light (love) from the car is directed in Judy's general direction, but she is separated from it. The car also moves toward the father, as Judy wishes her mother would do. Her dependency on the father is symbolized by the leaves, toward which she and her father are directing their attention. Judy initially placed father repairing the roof, but later added the leaves and "Dad."

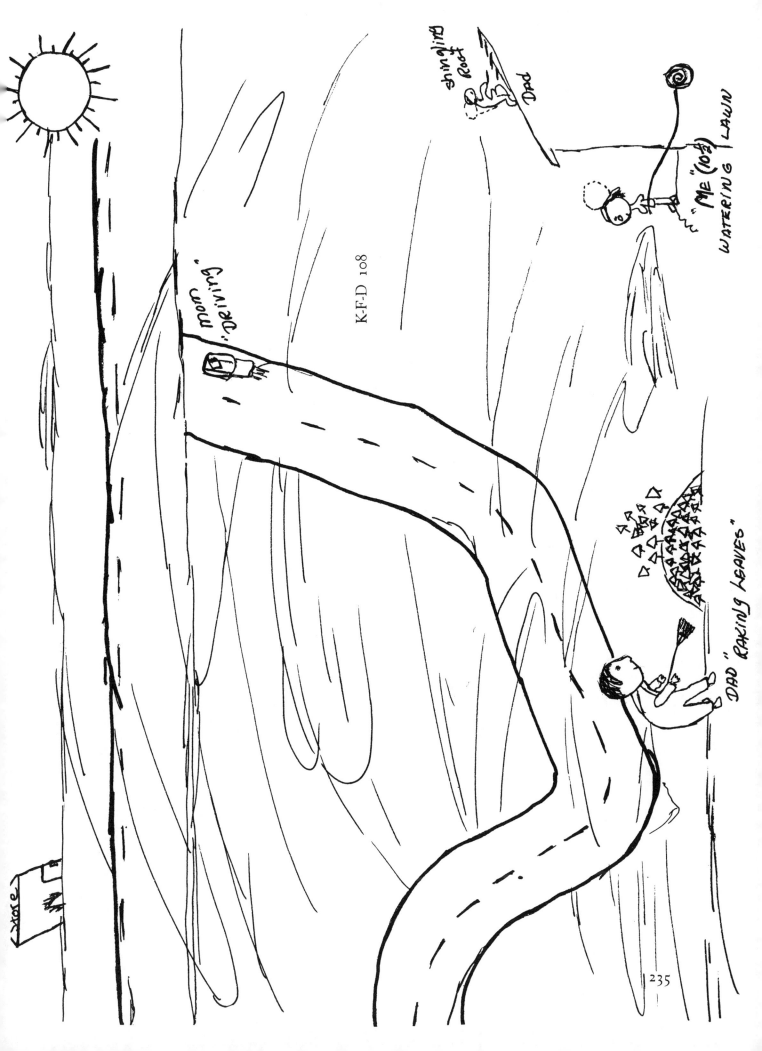

235

LEAVES (Cont.)

In some cases dependency needs are not met, and there is anger and ambivalence associated with these unmet needs.

K-F-D 109 was done by 9-year-old Susie, described as very dependent on her parents, particularly her father. She had dependency needs which were apparently not met. The burning leaves suggest the intensity of the feeling between Susie and her father, which at this stage of her development resulted from anger about unmet dependency needs.

"Burning Leaves"

Daddy

ME (9) STANDING

K-F-D 109

BROTHER (3) CRYING

Mother

"Playing ORGAN"

CRAIG (8) "HITTING"

LIGHT BULBS—Light bulbs serve as a symbol of the need for love and warmth. K-F-D 110, by 9-year-old Harry, shows him "putting the light bulb in." This is a family constellation in which both faceless parents are preoccupied with neatness and orderliness. There is very little warmth or love in the family, and Harry reflects this. Apparently he must obtain love (light) through his own activities.

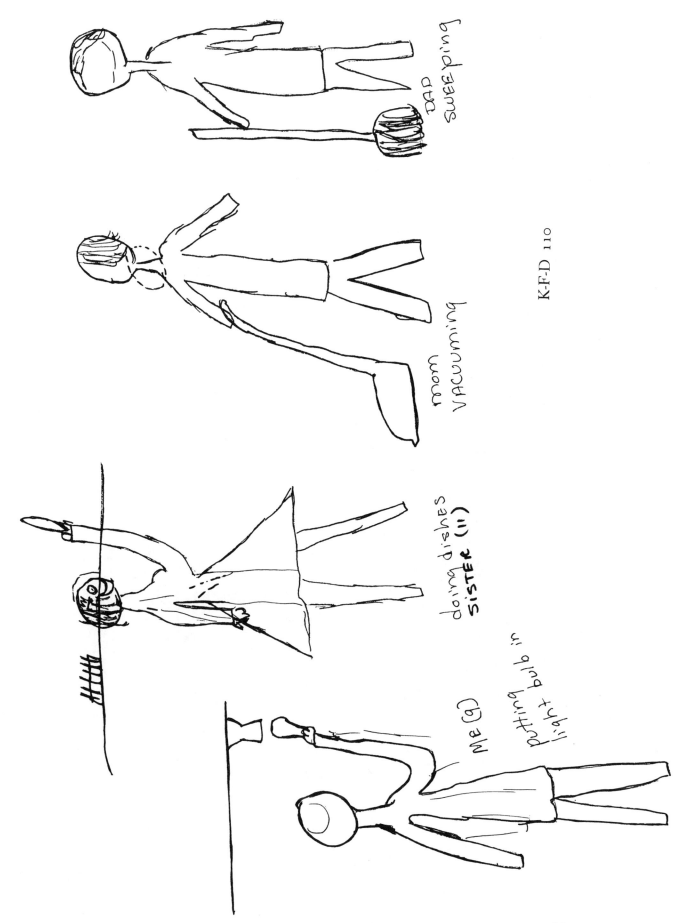

DAD
sweeping

mom
VACUUMING

K-F-D 110

doing dishes
SISTER (11)

Me (9)
putting bulb in
light bulb in

239

LIGHT BULBS (Cont.)

In K-F-D 111, by 10-year-old Ned, we see somewhat different dynamics. Ned's 14-year-old brother has been ill, and the family is very concerned about him. We note the encapsulation of the sick brother and the light above him reflecting the warmth and glow directed toward him. The angry expression and the shading of Ned's "Self" reflect, however, his anger and anxiety. There is significant ambivalence in his feeling toward his brother.

K-F-D 111

LIGHT BULBS (Cont.)

K-F-D 112, by 7½-year-old Greg, shows another use of the light bulb symbol. There is a new baby in the family, who, we note, has the ball-on-the-head (somewhat displaced), which reflects Greg's desire but inability to compete with him for love. In this case, the 9-year-old sister is seen as the nurturant person in the family. She has just given Greg a sandwich and is also holding a light bulb—the symbol of warmth. This sister tends to be very maternal and protective of Greg, and he is close to her. This is in contrast to his anger with the digging father and the distant mother.

Occasionally, the light bulb may be replaced by a similar symbol, such as a flashlight.

MoTHER
"Giving
out
Vegetables"

Dad
"Shovel
digging in
dirt"

K-F-D 112

Brother "Pushing his ball"

SiSTER (9)

"Sister bit
sandwich it - gave it to me cause
she did like it like I Did"

Light
Bulb

Me (7½)

243

LOGS—Logs are often associated with hypermasculinity or masculine striving. In K-F-D 113, by 8-year-old Gordon, the brother is carrying a log. This brother is dominant in the family, and Gordon sees him as a powerful and masculine figure.

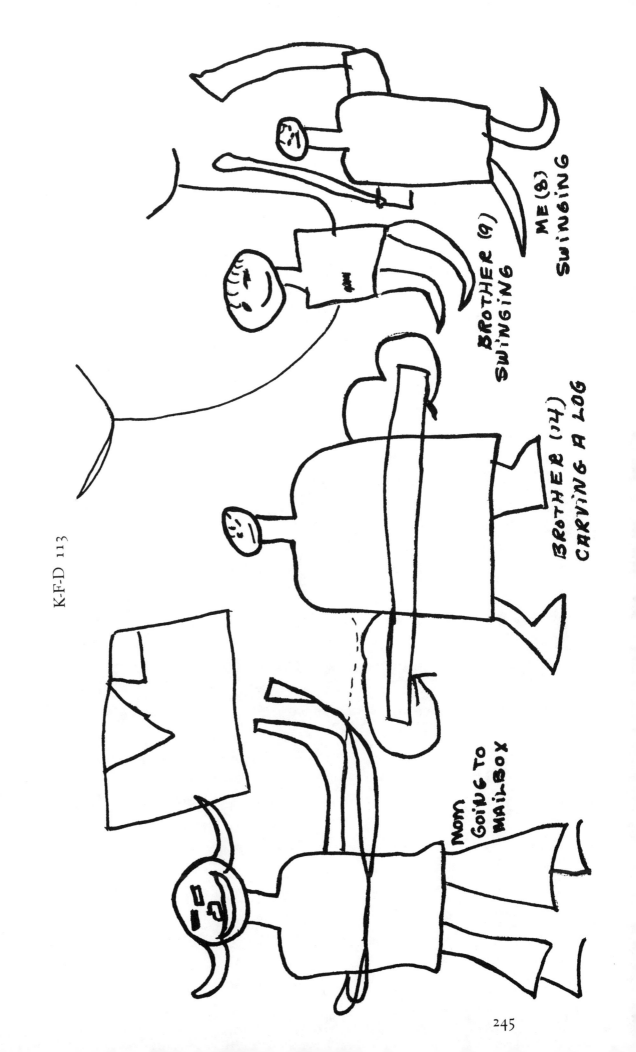

BROTHER (9)
SWINGING

ME (8)
SWINGING

BROTHER (14)
CARVING A LOG

Mom
GOING TO
MAILBOX

K-F-D 113

245

LOGS (Cont.)

In K-F-D 114, we see a similar theme with 12½-year-old Rick following in the footsteps of his older brother. They are both carrying logs, although the older brother has a much larger stack. Rick tags along and identifies with the older brother, and the logs appear to be associated with Rick's masculine strivings.

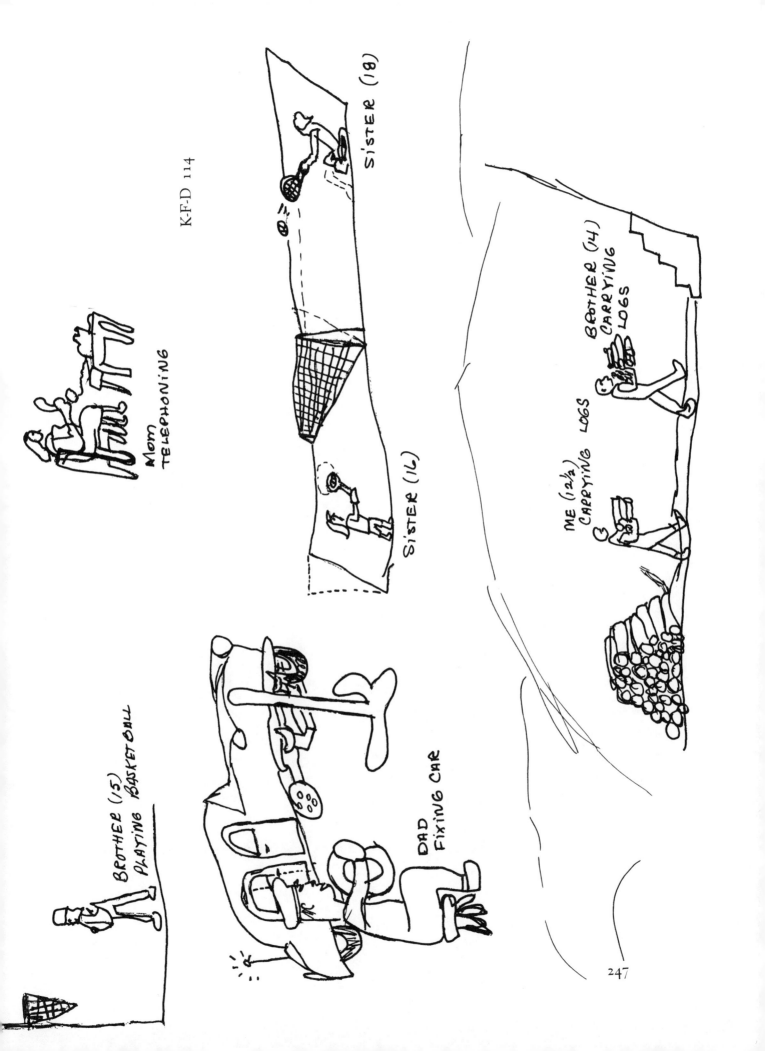

KF-D 114

SISTER (18)

SISTER (16)

BROTHER (14)
CARRYING LOGS

ME (12½)
CARRYING LOGS

Mom
TELEPHONING

BROTHER (15)
PLAYING BASKETBALL

DAD
FIXING CAR

PAINT BRUSH—The paint brush is often an extension of the hand and associated with a punishing figure. In K-F-D 115, 9-year-old John uses the paint brush as a symbol. John's father was physically very punishing. One notes his large size, his placement on the ladder, and the extension of the hand into the paint brush, which might also be a paddle. The father believed in physical punishment, and this boy had received many paddlings from him.

KF-D 115

249

RAIN—Rain is associated with depressive tendencies. There was much concern in the family of 8-year-old Jim, who did K-F-D 116, because of the father's depression. The father is encapsulated in the drawing and is walking in the rain. The father had had a number of periods of depression, and the boy was very eager to please him, hoping to make his father happier.

MOTHER
WatchiNg TV

K-F-D 116

DAD Going to store in the Rain

Brother(11) EATing
Dinner

ME(8) READiNg
Book

251

REFRIGERATORS—The refrigerator is associated with deprivation and depressive reactions to the deprivation. K-F-D 117 is by 7-year-old Jane, whose mother works. The mother is shown coming home from work, but she comes toward the refrigerator. The coldness from the refrigerator is opposite to the light or heat symbol. While the refrigerator is a source of nurturance, it is a basically cold object. The mother coming to the refrigerator reflects the child's nurturant needs. There are feelings of unmet dependency in relation to the mother. Note the compartmentalization in the drawing and the size and similarity of the father and the dog. The father is planting, and Jane is in the midst of her attempts to work through her closeness to her father. Identification with the mother is difficult with her working and out of the home.

Horses

"Dog"

mom

daddy

"Gardening"

K-F-D 117

MOM

"Refrigerator"

"coming from home from work"

SIS (11)

"DOING DISHES"

me

"going to ride bike" (9)

SKIN DIVING—An excessive interest in skin diving is associated with withdrawal and depressive tendencies, usually in the male. K-F-D 118 is fairly typical of teenage boys who have obsessive thoughts about skin diving. Thirteen-year-old Mike, who did this drawing, spent all of his spare time in this activity. Mike had a distant, preoccupied father. He felt emasculated; note the denial of the bottom half of the masculine figures. While he is talking on the phone, Mike's eyes are "glued" on the skin diving TV program.

When boys are questioned about this interest, they often say that under the water one cannot hear the parents. Boys who have intense preoccupations with skin diving are often distant from their fathers. They frequently feel emasculated and have depressive reactions to their feelings.

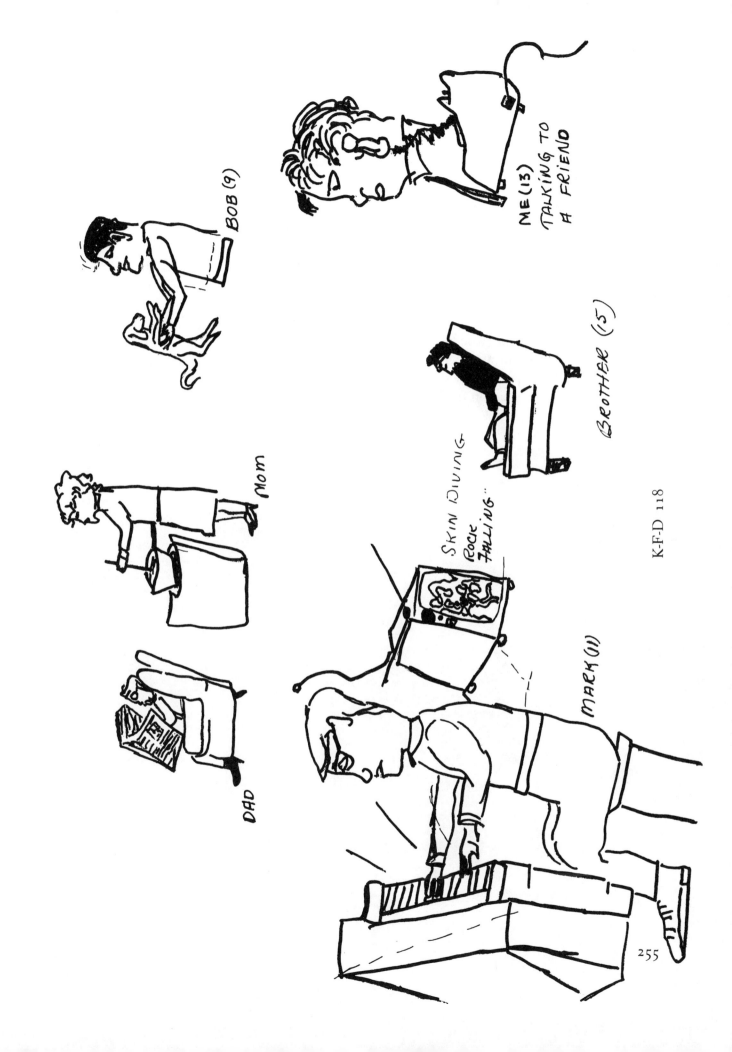

BOB (9)

ME (13)
TALKING TO
A FRIEND

BROTHER (5)

Mom

SKIN DIVING
"ROCK
FALLING"

DAD

MARK (11)

K·F·D 118

255

SNAKES—The snake as a phallic symbol is so well known in the literature that discussion of it is unnecessary. It is an infrequent symbol in the K-F-D population. K-F-D 119, however, shows one of the most frequent problems associated with preoccupation with the snake. This drawing was done by 10-year-old Norma, whose father was quite seductive. There was tension in the family, and Norma had a diagnosis of anxiety-hysteria. The snake is close to the father, who is shown making the bed. Norma has her back turned in an attempt to repress her sexual interest. In this case, the snake is associated with the father and Norma's fears and preoccupation in their sexualized relationship.

ME(10)

BACK

WASHING DISHES

a snack

SNAKE

a lizard

brother (5)

CRYING

father

MAKING HIS BED

My Dog
my Dog

a snail

brother (6)

YELLING

K-F-D 119

mother

DUSTING

257

STARS—This symbol is associated with deprivation (physical or emotional). Usually children associate stars with something cold and distant. Many children with histories of serious deprivation overexaggerate stars in a repetitive or compulsive way. Stars may occasionally be used to suggest pain, as in the comics.

In K-F-D 120, by 8-year-old Scott, who had a 6-month-old sibling, the mother is holding a star aloft. Scott is close to the mother but feels deprived. Note the cross-hatching around the baby. The star symbolizes Scott's depressive reaction to felt lack of maternal love. His 6-year-old sister also looks disgruntled.

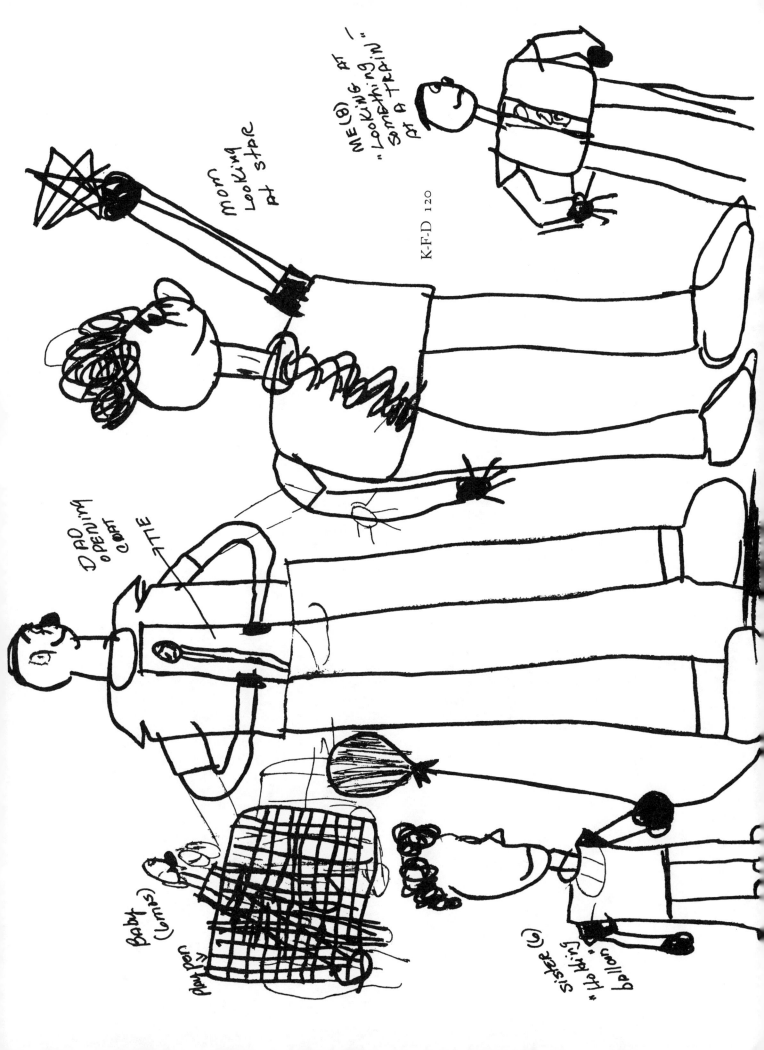

MoM Looking at stop

ME (8) - "Looking at something " At a TRAIN

K-F-D 120

DAD Opening COAT TTE

Baby (6mos)

play pen

Sister (6) "Hold on balloon"

STARS (Cont.)

Ten-year-old Billy, who had a very depressed mother, produced K-F-D 121. The mother is lying in bed and father's attention is focused upon "reaching" Mother. Note the compartmentalization and stars above Billy, reflecting his feelings of emotional deprivation.

MOM
SLEEPING

KF-D 121

SISTER (12)
COOKING

Dad

SISTER (6)
PLAYING WITH CAR

BROTHER (9)
RIDING BIKE

Me (10)

STARS (Cont.)

K-F-D 122 was made by Gus, 7 years old, a boy with a history of very serious physical deprivation. The table is the center of the picture and depicts his obsessive need for attention and food. Note the repetitive stars again, characteristic of children with histories of deprivation and usually a depressive reaction to this.

NOTHING

MOM
WASHING DISHES

TABLE

ME (7)
RIDING BIKE

DAD
FIXING CAR

BROTHER (9)
CLEANING BEDROOM

K-F-D 122

263

STOP SIGNS—Stop signs or "Keep Out" signs are obvious attempts at impulse control.

SUN—In younger children the drawing of the sun is extremely stereotyped and has little meaning, but occasionally, as children grow older, the drawing of the sun will have meaningful individual characteristics. For example, it may be darkened by depressed children. If given a face, the expression may be interpreted as are the expressions of the individual figure drawings. Children with a need for warmth and acceptance will often be facing or leaning toward the sun. Those with a feeling of rejection will often be far away from the sun, perhaps leaning away from it with their faces turned in the opposite direction.

TRAINS—Trains sometimes are power symbols with which children, especially boys, identify. This, of course, is quite normal in most children, but occasionally trains become an obsession.

In K-F-D's, undue interest in the train may be the prelude to a preoccupation and over-involvement with such power symbols as motorcycles, racing cars, etc. In K-F-D 123, we see an 11-year-old boy who depicts himself and his brother playing with an electric car set. It is noted that the line continues to the older brother on his motorbike. This is the drawing of a fairly normal boy who is going through a stage of development where he is seeking increasing power.

Brother (14)
Riding Bike

Brother (10)

Playing RACE
Cars with BROTHER

ME (11)

Mom
Cooking

Sister (14)

Watching
TV

K-F-D 123

265

TREES—Analysis of trees in drawings has been exhaustively described in the literature on the House-Tree-Person test (16). The symbolic meaning is greatly varied. For example, in K-F-D 124, an 11-year-old boy depicts the close relationship between father and mother as related to the growth process and they are "putting in a tree."

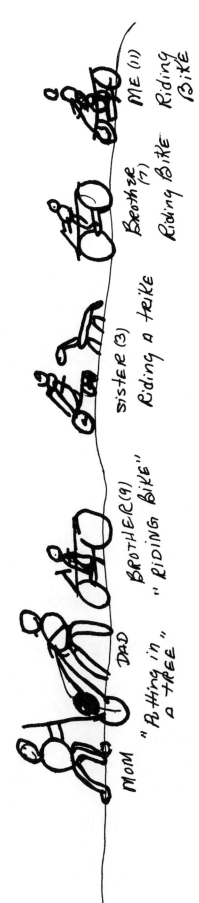

K-F-D 124

TREES (Cont.)

In K-F-D 125, we see the tree used in a very different way. Ten-year-old Dick, who produced this drawing, was an isolate. He felt extremely inadequate. The tree serves as a barrier between him and the rest of the family. He felt that the entire family belittled him, and he was quite emasculated by them. Note the cutting father mowing the lawn and the mother and older brother engaged in helping him by raking. The boy saw his father as a very threatening person and the mother and brother as aiding father in the cutting process. Even the younger sister and brother are helping in the cutting task. Dick remains tiny and isolated, protected from all this rivalry and threat by his tree.

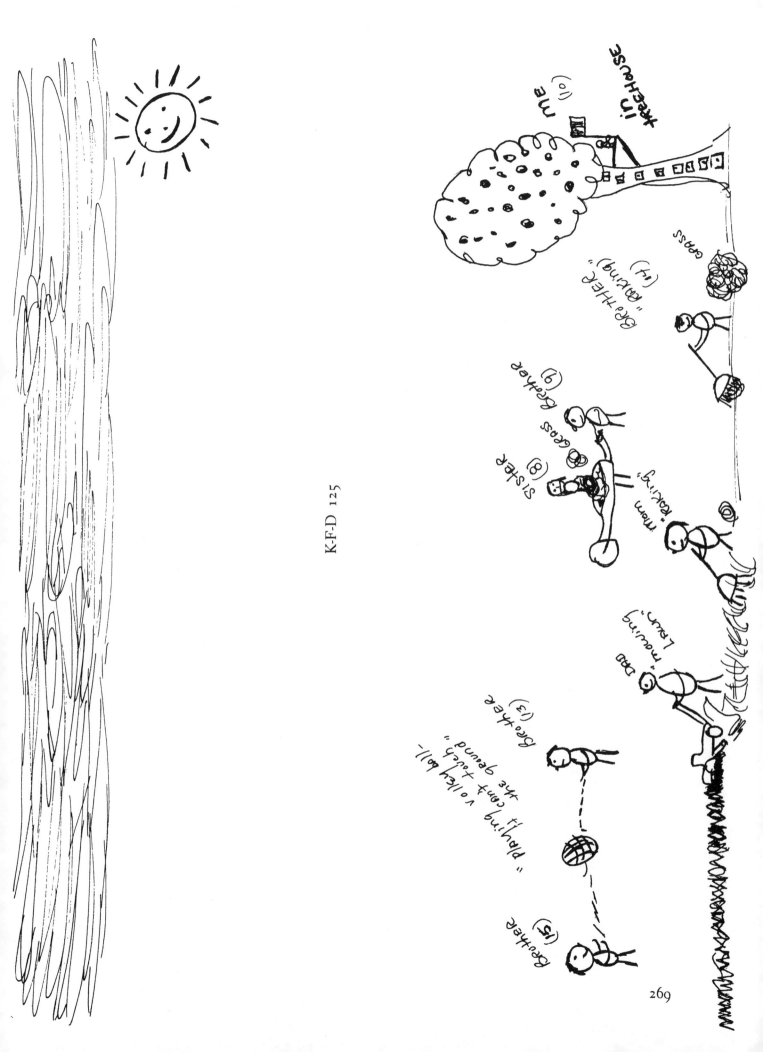

K-F-D 125

VACUUMS—Vacuums are symbols of powerful, controlling, "sucking-up," cleaning devices. The mothers using them are often viewed in the same way.

There may be other members of the family constellation who fit this role. K-F-D 126, by 5-year-old Lisa, shows the grandmother vacuuming. This was, indeed, a very domineering grandmother who controlled her own daughter as well as her grandchild. Note the size of the grandmother in comparison to the mother. Even at age 5, Lisa has shut herself off from this control by compartmentalizing and is angrily pounding on the roof.

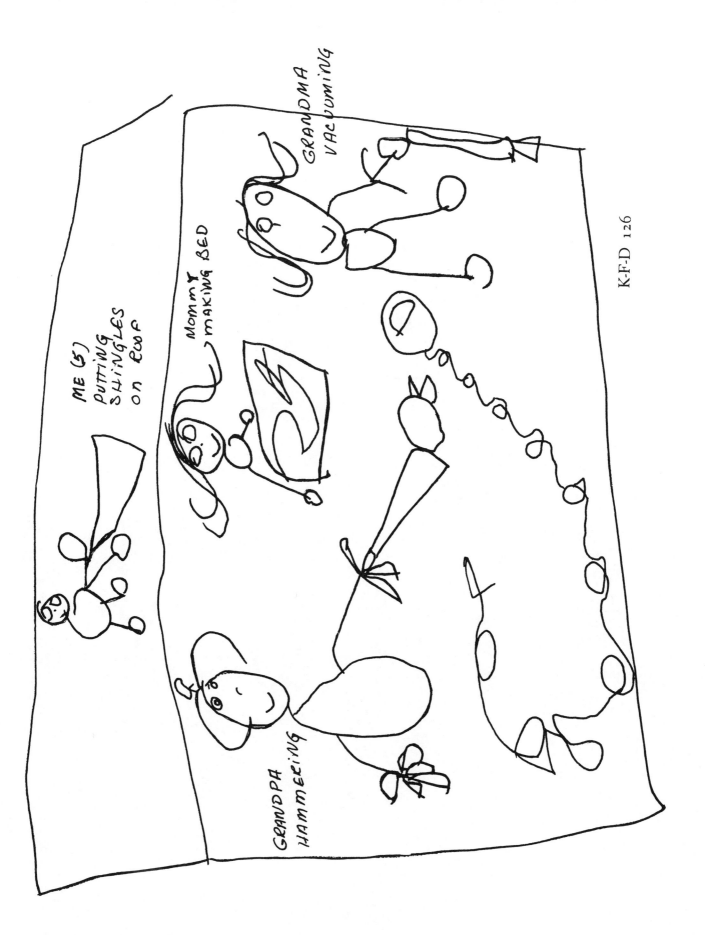

GRANDMA VACUUMING

MOMMY MAKING BED

ME (5) PUTTING SHINGLES ON ROOF

GRANDPA HAMMERING

K-F-D 126

271

VACUUMS (Cont.)

In K-F-D 127, done by 10-year-old Mary, who has a great deal of difficulty in school, we notice the vacuum's size and position where it might suck the child in. Note the child having difficulty in school is centered between two "A"'s, which reflect the mother's great academic hopes for her child.

BROTHER (18)
READING

SISTER (16)
WASHING

MOM
VACUUMING

SELF (10)

K-F-D 127

273

VACUUMS (Cont.)

In K-F-D 128, Sarah, age 9, is the oldest girl in a family with an extremely controlling mother. Note the size of the vacuuming mother, who is viewing the entire family and perhaps controlling them. Sarah, at the time she drew this, was attempting to identify with the father. One sees, however, that she places herself on a pedestal along with the father in some hope of being as big as her overpowering, controlling mother.

The faces of the mother and daughter are quite similar, and one suspects that as Sarah grows older she will identify with the mother and her controlling devices, perhaps becoming a controlling mother herself some day.

K-F-D 128

Mom
"vacuum-
ing"

Dad
"Playing
ball"

stool

"Playing
Ball"

Me (9)

Bench

Ball

Kris
(8)

Dusting

DENNIS (5)

DRAWING

WATER—Over-exaggeration and preoccupation with water is associated with depression. Often there will be a floating figure in the drawing and usually there are significant depressive themes associated with this figure.

K-F-D 129 was produced by 11-year-old Tom, who was referred because of his depression. This boy was capable of drawing much more mature figures. In the family he also acted much younger. Tom had been the baby of the family for 8 years and resented giving up the "baby" role. One notes the rotated baby at the top and the ominous older brother. The father and mother are threatening, "cutting" figures. We see Tom closest to his 3-year-old sister. Tom had often identified with her. Note that she is in the swimming pool and Tom is carrying water.

KEVIN (14)
MOWING LAWN

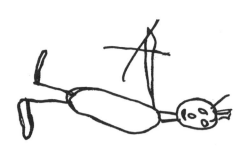

BABY STANDING UP

BABY

K-F-D 129

o o MOM
CUTTING CARROTS

DAD

CHOPPING WOOD

SISTER (3)
FILLING UP
HER SWIMMING
POOL

SELF (11)
GETTING
WATER OFF
THE WOOD

277

WATER (Cont.)

In more serious depressive situations, we see greater preoccupation with the water. For example, in K-F-D 130, we have a family in which there is a seriously depressed mother who has attempted suicide on three occasions. Ten-year-old Brian could only draw his head with the rest of the body immersed in water. The mother has her back turned to the family and has her own preoccupations as she looks at the lake. The father is seen as cutting and threatening, but the dominant and central part of the picture is the water, with Brian plaintively watching his mother, who has her back turned to the family.

Mom
LOOKING AT THE LAKE

DAD
MOWING LAWN

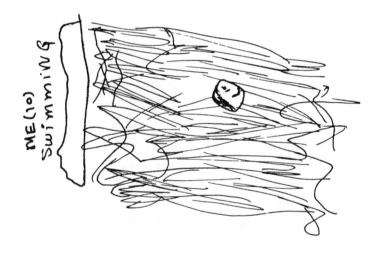

ME (10)
Swimming

K-F-D 130

BROTHER (6)
SLiDING ON
BANNISTER

WATER (Cont.)

In K-F-D 131, we have a 13-year-old boy who is quite distant from the father. Larry is described by others as a "loner." His parents thought him depressed. He has his back turned to the family, especially the father, who is far distant in the picture and faced in the opposite direction. The boy is sitting in the same position as the younger children in the family, thus showing some regressive tendencies, but primarily a depressive reaction, as he depicts himself near the water.

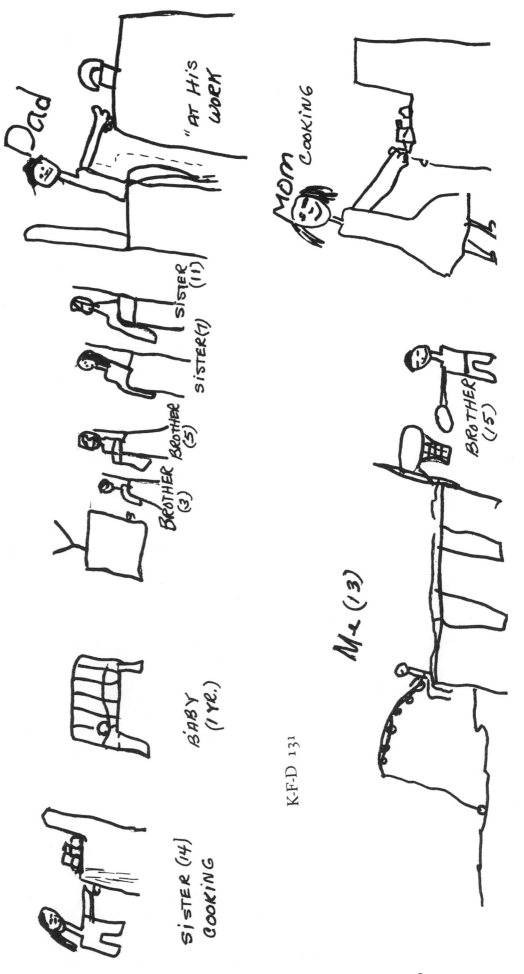

Dad
"AT HIS WORK"

Mom
COOKING

SISTER (11)
SISTER (7)

BROTHER (5)
BROTHER (3)

BABY (1 YR.)

SISTER (14)
COOKING

BROTHER (15)

M+ (3)

K-F-D 131

WATER (Cont.)

K-F-D 132, by 11-year-old Molly, shows the "Self" isolated and in water. Molly was referred because of depressive feelings. She often dreamed she was sinking in water. Her 3-year-old brother was retarded and the center of the family's attention.

DAD READING NEWSPAPER

MOM COOKING

K-F-D 132

ME (11) Swimming

Sister (13) Folding Clothes from DRYER

Brother (12) (Retarded) ON TABLE BEING patterned

Brother (3) playing piano

WATER (Cont.)

In K-F-D 133, a 12-year-old boy depicts his extreme pre-occupation with water. This was discussed in some detail under Skin Diving. Nick, however, presents a gross preoccupation, with withdrawal symptoms beginning a depressive-like reaction. There is a distance from the threatening parents, particularly the mother. The floating quality of all of the persons in the drawing was quite similar to the floaty, schizoid adjustment of 12-year-old Nick. He felt, in his fantasy, that the underwater life was much safer. His total mood was depressed. Note his face turned away from the others and his total fixation and preoccupation with the "Voyage to the Bottom of the Sea."

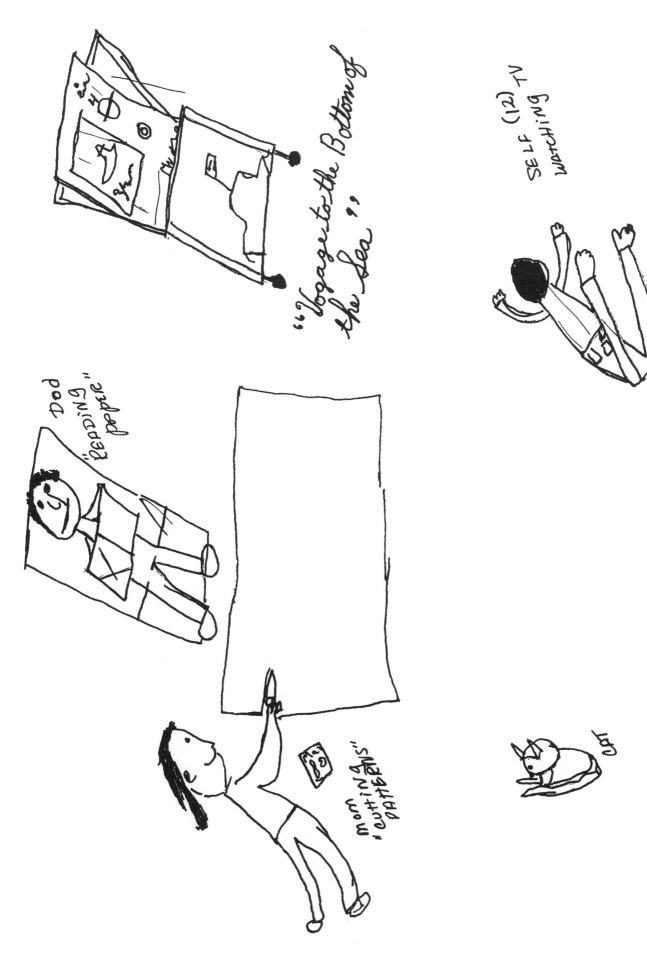

"Voyage to the Bottom of the Sea"

SELF (12) watching TV

Dod "Reading" paper

Mom "Cutting" PATTERNS

CAT

K-F-D 133

CHAPTER 7

K-F-D GRID AND
ANALYSIS
SHEET

In addition to the analysis of K-F-D actions, styles and symbols, we have found it helpful to use a simple K-F-D grid and analysis sheet.

A.   K-F-D GRID

A grid made of tracing paper marked off in millimeters has proven useful in obtaining certain K-F-D data. By superimposing the grid over a K-F-D, a number of measurements may be made.

The grid may be of help in obtaining the measurements of the Self and other K-F-D figures. The distance of the Self from the other figures is also at times very important.

The location of the Self and the other figures on the grid may also be of interest. For example, conditions such as "superiority" or "inferiority" complex may be defined in terms of the size of the Self and placement on the grid.

Such measurements may be of value in studying the individual as his own control or in studying the differences between intra- or inter-cultural variables.

B.   K-F-D ANALYSIS SHEET

A simple analysis sheet has been of help in summarizing and recording data. Measurements derived from K-F-D 134 may serve as an example.

Bill, who produced K-F-D 134, was undergoing acute family pressures. His parents had recently been divorced and the mother had remarried. The stepfather was reaching out for Bill, but the boy was unsure of his feelings. The true father had severe problems of which Bill was aware. Bill's great stress and struggles are well portrayed by him in his K-F-D and by the salient features summarized in the K-F-D analysis sheet.

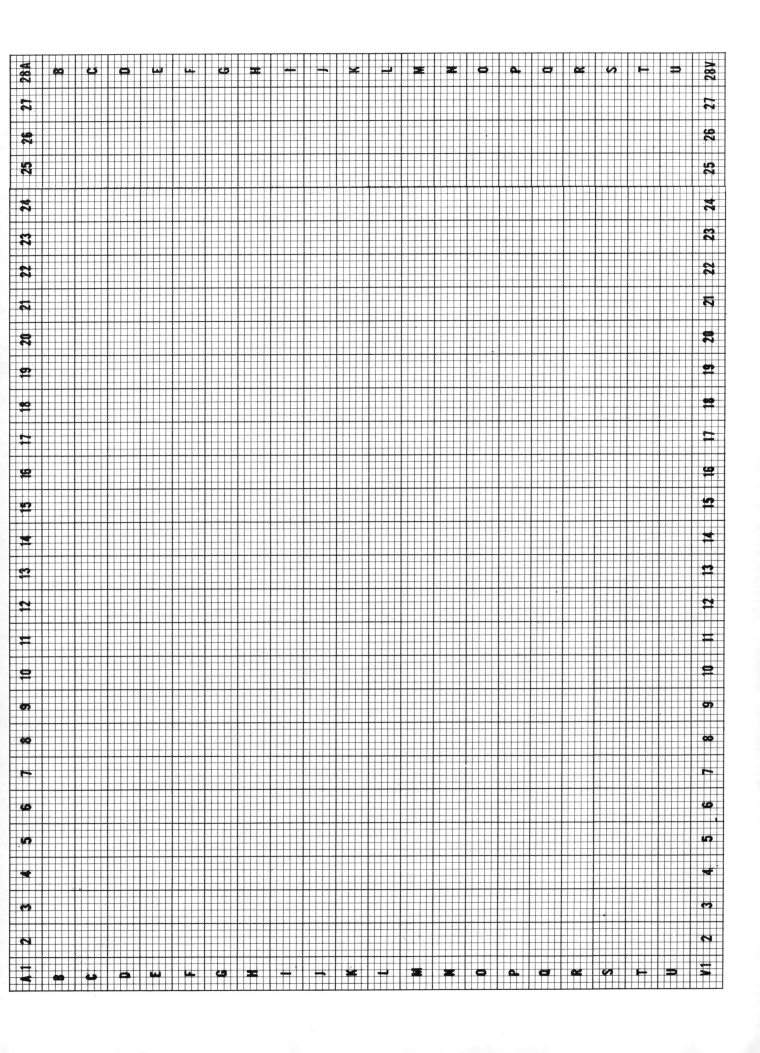

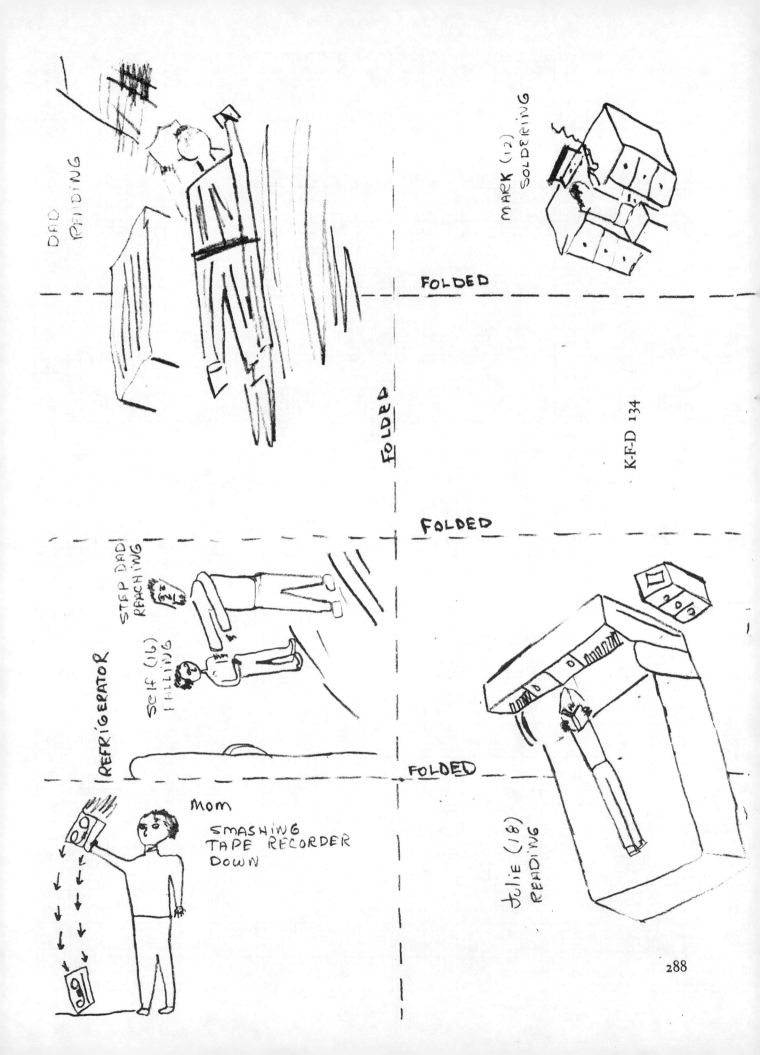

DAD READING

MARK (12) SOLDERING

FOLDED

FOLDED

K-F-D 134

FOLDED

STEP DAD REACHING

Self (16) FALLING

REFRIGERATOR

FOLDED

Julie (18) READING

Mom

SMASHING TAPE RECORDER DOWN

288

K-F-D ANALYSIS SHEET

Name: _Bill_ Age: _16_ Sex: _M_

I. STYLE(s) (Circle)
A. Compartmentalization
B. Edging
C. Encapsulation
(D.) Folded Compartmentalization
E. Lining on the Bottom
F. Lining on the Top
G. Underlining Individual Figures

II. SYMBOL(s)
A. _Refrigerator_ D. ___
B. ___ E. ___
C. ___ F. ___

III. (A) ACTIONS OF INDIVIDUAL FIGURES

Figure	Action
1. Self	_Falling_
2. Mother	_laughing_
3. Father	_reaching_
4. Older Brother	_-_
5. Older Sister	_resting_
6. Younger Brother	_holding_
7. Younger Sister	_-_
8. Other (Specify)	_reaching_
Step-dad	

(B) ACTIONS BETWEEN INDIVIDUAL FIGURES

Figure	Action	Recipient
1. Self	_Falling_	_step-dad_
2. Mother	_laughing_	_step-mom_
3. Father		
4. O.B.		
5. O.S.		
6. Y.B.		
7. Y.S.		
8. Other (Spec)	_step-dad_ _reaching_	_self_

IV. CHARACTERISTICS OF INDIVIDUAL K-F-D FIGURES

A. Arm Extensions
1. Self   5. O.S.
(2.) Mother (6.) Y.B.
(3.) Father 7. Y.S.
4. O.B.   (8.) Other

B. Elevated Figures
(1.) Self   5. O.S.
2. Mother   6. Y.B.
3. Father   7. Y.S.
4. O.B.   8. Other

C. Erasures
1. Self   5. O.S.
2. Mother   6. Y.B.
3. Father   7. Y.S.
4. O.B.   8. Other

D. Figures on Back
1. Self   5. O.S.
2. Mother   6. Y.B.
3. Father   7. Y.S.
4. O.B.   8. Other

E. Hanging
(1.) Self   5. O.S.
2. Mother   6. Y.B.
3. Father   7. Y.S.
4. O.B.   8. Other

F. Omission of Body Parts
(1.) Self   5. O.S.
2. Mother   (6.) Y.B.
3. Father   7. Y.S.
4. O.B.   8. Other

G. Omission of Figures
1. Self   5. O.S.
2. Mother   6. Y.B.
3. Father   7. Y.S.
4. O.B.   8. Other

H. Picasso Eye
1. Self   5. O.S.
2. Mother   6. Y.B.
3. Father   7. Y.S.
4. O.B.   8. Other

I. Rotated Figures
1. Self   5. O.S.
(2.) Mother 6. Y.B.
3. Father   7. Y.S.
4. O.B.   8. Other

V. K-F-D GRID

A. Height
1. Self _7 cm._   5. O.S. _5 in._
2. M _6 "_   6. Y.B. _3 "_
3. F _7.5 "_   7. Y.S. _-_
4. O.B. _-_   8. Other _7 "(step-dad)_

B. Location of Self

C. Distance of Self from:
Mother _3.5 in._
Father _"_
Other (Specify) _0_
step-dad

Folded compartmentalization, the style selected by Bill, reflects the severity of the boy's conflict and his desperate defense against the stresses associated with the loss of the father, the anger and distortion in relation to the mother, and the attempts to establish a new relationship with the stepfather.

The refrigerator as a symbol, placed between himself and his mother, reflects Bill's feelings of depression and loss of love.

In the actions of the various figures, Bill reflects his tension and anger. For example, in the Self depicted as falling, one has a feeling of the great tension which is present throughout the K-F-D. The mother is smashing—reflecting the boy's anger with her for disrupting the family. The Dad and older sister are reading, but in so doing their faces are hidden, and this is part of Bill's defense of intellectualization which he uses so effectively in conversation. The younger brother also has his face averted and is soldering. Perhaps some of the warmth that the boy needs is associated with his brother, who is, indeed, a warm little boy and one to whom Bill can relate.

In the actions between the figures, however, we see the boy falling away from the stepfather. In some ways, he has a great deal of guilt in establishing a relationship with the stepfather, as Bill feels that he will then be disloyal to his own father, whom he visits each week.

The mother is actually quite a gentle, but firm, person, yet, Bill tends to attribute much of the problem to her. Thus, his own anger is depicted in her smashing the inanimate object.

The stepfather is reaching for Bill, and Bill apparently feels and is trying to accept this attempt to establish a warm relationship. One notes the arm extensions of the stepfather as he reaches toward the boy.

We have more subtle arm extensions with the mother, the father and the brother, as well as the sister. These are related to Bill's great striving and need to control the environment. He has high levels of aspiration, and all of his figures have some ways to control the environment. This is in contrast to himself, who at the present time feels rather helpless—he actually has only one arm.

We note, however, that he has elevated himself to a height close to that of the stepfather. He is near the top of the paper, reflecting his desire to be dominant.

While there are minimal erasures, one notes that the mother's eyes have been erased. Bill respects her and gets much of his control from her. However, at the present time, he has great ambivalence toward his mother and conflict in accepting her controls.

The rotation of the mother on the paper is significant and is related to Bill's views of a topsy-turvy world in which his relation to everyone, including a primary relationship to the mother, is distorted at the present time.

In terms of the size of the figures, we note that the largest size by far is that of the true father. Bill has numerous obsessive thoughts about his well-being and great conflict and preoccupation with the father. It is noted that the stepfather and the mother are about the same size and larger than the Self.

Bill draws himself far distant from the true father, as well as showing the compartmentalization between them. There is less distance between Bill and the mother. There is a zero distance between the stepfather and Bill. This reflects Bill's attempts at acceptance and establishing a normal and warm relationship to "step-Dad."

Thus, our K-F-D analysis sheet allows us to summarize and partially quantify some of the actions, styles and symbols of Bill's K-F-D.

The grid and analysis sheet are especially helpful in longitudinal studies of children in evaluating such variables as psychotherapy or environmental manipulation.

Consider the drawings of Jack, age 11. In K-F-D 135, Jack portrayed his "home" with his true mother. The mother had been hospitalized on four occasions for mental illness. She had been extremely violent and had beaten Jack on numerous occasions. The stepfather was also mentally ill and violent.

Jack isolates and encapsulates himself in an effort to protect himself from the deranged parents. He has no face. Note the size of the Self (1 cm.) and the distortions in the drawing.

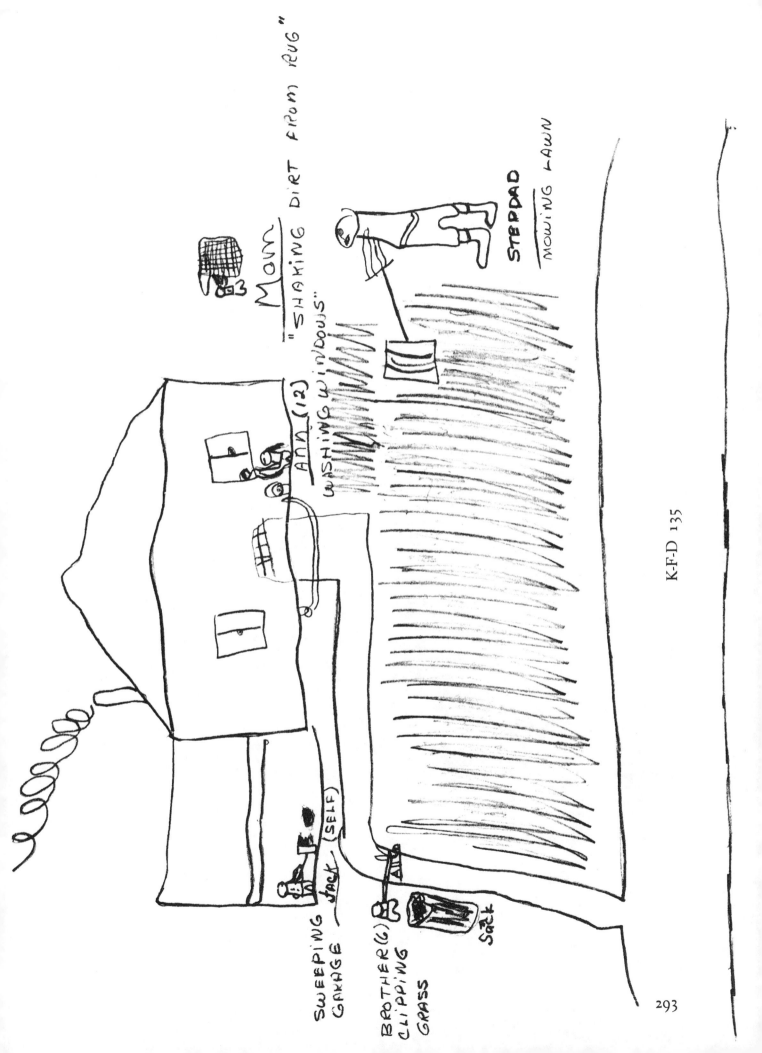

Mom
"SHAKING DIRT FROM RUG"

STEPDAD
MOWING LAWN

ANN (12)
WASHING WINDOWS

SWEEPING
GARAGE   Jack (SELF)

BROTHER (6)
CLIPPING
GRASS   Jack

K-F-D 135

293

Jack had begged to live with the true father and this was finally arranged. Three months after moving into his new home, Jack produced K-F-D 136.

Note the lack of barriers in Jack's new family constellation. The increase in size of the Self (5 cm.) is striking. Jack has many problems to overcome, but in his new environment his "Self-confidence" has increased. He can "communicate" with his new parents without artificial barriers. Jack now has a face and freedom to grow.

BASEBALL
"CATCHING"

JACK (11)
——————
SELF

ANDY (1½)
——————
PLAYING XYLOPHONE

K-F-D 136

MOM
——————
WASHING DISHES

DAD
——————
MOWING LAWN

295

CHAPTER 8

CONCLUSION

The purpose of this book has been to summarize the actions, styles and symbols depicted by children and adolescents in their Kinetic Family Drawings.

The K-F-D actions are relatively simple to observe and to reliably record.

A few styles are easily recognizable; yet, many are not decipherable. We note the lack of "style" in the K-F-D's of normal children and the obvious "style" (such as, folded compartmentalization) of severely disturbed children. Thus "styles" resemble "defense mechanisms." Lack of style suggests a diminished need for defense. Perhaps defense mechanisms, such as, denial, regression, isolation, etc., should be included as "styles." Much more work is obviously needed in observing and recording "styles."

The observation and interpretation of symbols is even more difficult and subject to interpreter and cultural distortions. Yet, understanding the condensed "meaning" of a symbol often reveals the "heart" of the child's conflict, as indicated in K-F-D 1, which is where we began our discussion and where we reluctantly end.

APPENDIX

CLINICAL INTERPRETATION OF FEATURES IN INDIVIDUAL HUMAN FIGURE DRAWINGS

ARMS—Controllers of the physical environment. Thus, when arms are long and powerful, they are reaching out to control the environment. Lack of arms suggests a feeling of helplessness.

ARMS, FOLDED—Usually produced by suspicious and hostile persons.

BELT, HEAVILY EMPHASIZED—Suggests conflict between expression and control of sex or impulse.

BILATERAL SYMMETRY—If overemphasized denotes an obsessive-compulsive system of emotional control.

BUTTONS—Dependency. In many profile drawings of young children, the relation between buttons and breasts is obvious, as in Drawing 137, done by Billy, a very babyish 7-year-old boy. (See next page.)

BROAD SHOULDERS—Need for physical power.

CARTOONS, CLOWN FIGURES—Self-depreciating attitude. Defensive.

CROSS-HATCHING—Attempts to control anxiety through obsessive-compulsive methods.

DISPROPORTIONATELY SMALL BODY PARTS—Feelings of inadequacy in the specific areas. Also, denial or repression; for example, eyes very small or absent are often related to denial of function in the visual area.

MOM HOLDING ME

ME (4)

K-F-D 137

DAD

OLDER SISTER (15)

EARS—Disturbances or distortion of the ear may mean anything from a mild sensitivity to social criticism to systematized paranoia. Distortion of the form of the ear, marked displacement, or odd detailing and "activity" in the ear usually reflect psychopathology. Hearing loss or history of hearing loss should also be considered.

ERASURES—Conflict or denial.

EXAGGERATION OF BODY PARTS—Preoccupation with the function of these parts.

EYES—Facial features refer primarily to social communication. Large eyes may scan the world for information, while small or closed eyes may exclude it. They may be paranoid in their wariness, or crossed out in guilt for what they have seen.

FACIAL EXPRESSION—Facial expressions depicting various emotions are felt to be one of the more reliable signs in H-F-D's, according to Machover.

FEET, LONG—Need for security.

FEET, TINY—Dependence, constriction.

LONG NECKS—Usually reflect dependency in children's drawings. Because the neck connects the impulse-laden body with the controlling mind, the neck is a frequent area of conflict expression.

MOUTH—Mouth emphasis may be associated with feeding difficulties or speech disturbances. In children, overemphasis is most frequently associated with dependency.

OMISSION OF BODY PARTS—Suggests denial of function.

PRECISION, ORDERLINESS, NEATNESS—Often reflect a child's concern or need for a structured environment. Over-concern with structure may be viewed as an attempt to control a threatening environment.

PRESSURE—The pressure used in producing a drawing suggests outward or inward direction of impulse, i.e., the depressed person presses lightly; the aggressive, acting-out individual uses excessive pressure.

SHADING OR SCRIBBLING—Shading in a drawing suggests preoccupation, fixation or anxiety.

SIZE—The size of a drawing suggests a diminished or exaggerated view of the Self. The person who feels very inadequate usually draws a tiny Person.

TEETH, PROMINENT—Anger.

This list is meant to be only a brief introduction to analysis of individual human figure drawings. A more complete evaluation may be obtained by referring to works such as those of Machover (19) (20).

REFERENCES

1. ALSCHULER, R. H. and HATTWICK, L. W.: Painting and Personality, A Study of Young Children (2 Vols.). University of Chicago Press, Chicago, Ill. 1947.

2. ANASTASI, A. and FOLEY, J. P., Jr.: "A survey of the literature on artistic behavior in the abnormal. III. Spontaneous productions." *Psychol. Monogr.*, 1940, 52, 71 ff.

3. BENDER, L.: "Art and therapy in the mental disturbances of children." *J. Nerv. Ment. Dis.*, 1937, 86, 249-263.

4. BUCK, J. N.: The H-T-P Technique: A Qualitative and Quantitative Scoring Manual, *J. Clin. Psychol.* 4: 317-396. 1948.

5. BURNS, R. C. and KAUFMAN, S. H.: Kinetic Family Drawings (K-F-D): An Introduction to Understanding Children through Kinetic Drawings. Brunner/Mazel, New York, N. Y. 1970.

6. BURNS, R. C.: Movement: Key to Understanding Intelligence of the Special Child in Century 21. In Jerome Hellmuth (Ed.), The Special Child in Century 21, Special Child Publications, Seattle, Wash. 1964.

7. DENNIS, WAYNE: Group Values Through Children's Drawings. John Wiley and Sons. New York, N. Y. 1966.

8. DESPERT, J. L.: Emotional Problems in Children. New York: New York State Hospitals Press. 1938.

9. Di LEO, J. H.: Young Children and Their Drawings. Brunner/Mazel, New York, N. Y. 1970.

10. FENICHEL, O.: The Psychoanalytic Theory of Neurosis. Norton, New York, N. Y. 1945.

11. FREUD, SIGMUND: The Interpretation of Dreams. In Brill, A. H. (Ed.), The Basic Writings of Sigmund Freud. New York, N. Y. Modern Library, 1938, 181-549.

12. GOODENOUGH, F. L.: Measurement of Intelligence by Drawings. World Book Company, Yonkers, N. Y. 1926.

13. HAMMER, E. F.: The Clinical Application of Projective Drawings. Charles C Thomas, Springfield, Ill. 1958.

14. HULSE, W. C.: The Emotionally Disturbed Child Draws His Family. *Quart. J. Child Behavior*. 3:152-174. 1951.

15. HULSE, W. C.: Child Conflict Expressed Through Family Drawings. *J. Proj. Tech.* 16:66-79. 1952.

16. JOLLES, ISAAC: A Catalogue for the Qualitative Interpretation of the House-Tree-Person (H-T-P). Western Psychological Services, Beverly Hills, California. 1964.

17. KOPPITZ, E. M.: Psychological Evaluation of Children's Human Figure Drawings. Grune and Stratton, Inc., New York, N. Y. 1968.

18. LEWIN, K.: Psychoanalysis and Topological Psychology. *Bull. Menninger Clin.*, 1:202-211. 1937.

19. MACHOVER, K.: Human Figure Drawings of Children. *J. Proj. Tech.* 17:85-91. 1953.

20. MACHOVER, K.: Personality Projection in the Drawing of the Human Figure. Charles C Thomas. Springfield, Ill. 1949.

21. RAVEN, J. C.: Controlled Projection for Children. K. K. Lewis & Co. Ltd., London. 1951.

22. REZNIKOFF, M. A. and REZNIKOFF, H. R.: The Family Drawing Test: A comparative study of children's drawings. *J. Clin. Psychol.*, 12:167-169. 1956.

23. SHEARN, C. R. and RUSSELL, K. R.: Use of the Family Drawing as a Technique for Studying Parent-Child Interaction. *J. of Proj. Tech. & Person. Assess.*, Vol. 33, No. 1. 1969.

24. SKINNER, B. F.: The Behavior of Organisms. D. Appleton-Century. New York, N. Y. 1938.

INDEX